"Storyboarding 101 even motivated me to pick up a pencil."
William J. Miller,
Walt Disney Studios

"Storyboarding 101 is brilliant! I was drawing within ten minutes!"
Patty Arima Cheung,
Independent Filmmaker

"Storyboarding 101 is a true survival guide for any artist attempting to set foot in Hollywood."
David Michael Wieger,
Writer, Wild America for Morgan Creek and Warner Bros

"I highly recommend Storyboarding 101 for anyone seriously considering storyboarding as their profession."
Christopher Caris,
Producer, Academy Award nominated, At the Edge of Conquest

D0967304

STORYBOARDING 101

A CRASH COURSE IN PROFESSIONAL STORYBOARDING

BY

JAMES O. FRAIOLI

Published by Michael Wiese Productions, 11288 Ventura Blvd., Suite 821,
Studio City, CA 91604, (818) 379-8799 Fax (818) 986-3408.
E-mail: wiese@mwp.com
www.mwp.com

Cover design by The Art Hotel
Interior design and layout by Patti Halstead

Printed by McNaughton & Gunn, Inc., Saline, Michigan
Manufactured in the United States of America
Copyright © 2000 by James O. Fraioli

All rights reserved. No part of this book may be reproduced in any form or by any means without permission in writing from the publisher, except for the inclusion of brief quotations in a review.

Library of Congress Cataloging-in-Publication Data

Fraioli, James O., 1968 -
        Storyboarding 101: A crash course in professional storyboarding/
        by James O. Fraioli.
            p. cm.
        Includes bibliographical references.
        ISBN 0-941188-25-6
        1. Storyboards. 2. Commercial art – Vocational guidance – United States. I. Title:
        Storyboarding one hundred one. II. Title: Storyboarding one hundred and one.
        III. Title.

        NC1002.S85 F73 2000
        741.5'8 – dc21   00-025402

Dedication

This book is dedicated to my family:

Mom, Pop & Tanya

Thanks for everything.

STORYBOARDING 101
BY JAMES O. FRAIOLI

TABLE OF CONTENTS

INTRODUCTION

A Brief Introduction

Welcome to the pursuit of an exciting career in storyboarding. If you are looking for a golden opportunity which combines artistry and the thrill of the entertainment business, becoming a storyboard artist is for you. Storyboard artists are always in high demand and are basically used behind the scenes in virtually every movie you see on the silver screen. Your desire to be working with high-profile directors, producers, production designers, actors and actresses can also become a reality as a storyboard artist. So what are you waiting for? Opportunity awaits you!

I wrote Storyboarding 101 for the purpose of helping those who aspire to become storyboard artists but don't know where to start. When I began, I knew nothing about storyboards. I never took an art class, and I didn't even know how to seek a career in the field. Yet, after several months, I suddenly found myself immersed in storyboards while working on my very first movie. Six months later, I moved to Hollywood and took a job with the Walt Disney Studio; and a year later, I was storyboarding for top directors in Hollywood. The bottom line is that if I can do it, you can do it.

There are many ways of breaking into the storyboard arena of the entertainment business. Talking with many fellow artists, I found that each one of them seemed to have a slightly different story. As you read this book, please keep in mind that everything I am advising is based solely on my own personal experiences. You may follow any direction you prefer, but based on my accomplishments and years of experience, I feel I can offer you a pretty solid game plan for ultimately succeeding in a very competitive industry. Take it for what it's worth. And good luck!

- James O. Fraioli

PART I
YOUR BLANK
SHEET OF PAPER

Chapter One

WHERE TO BEGIN?

That is the same question I asked myself one lazy morning after my parents barked at me to get out of bed and find a "real" job. I had graduated from the University of Southern California, a prestigious and highly ranked film school in the country, but instead of using my hard-earned (and expensive) degree, I found myself living back at home while working landscaping and construction jobs. In other words, I didn't have a clue about what I wanted to do after college. I just knew I needed some money to get by and I had to make enough so I could eventually move out of the house. Thinking back on those days, I guess I wasn't ready to tackle life after school, or just not aware of what the working world had to offer. After all, I had been pretty sheltered behind those walls at USC, not to mention having been distracted by never-ending college.

Yes, it was time to get myself out of bed and dive into a career which would motivate me to get up in the morning and make me proud of myself when I looked in the mirror. But what was that career going to be?

While I delved into the endless possibilities of serious employment (which bought me time to score some free rent off mom and dad), I decided I wanted to do something in the creative, artistic field, an area I always enjoyed. At that time, a motion picture, American Heart, starring Jeff Bridges, was shooting in town. Curious, and always having a fascination for the movies, I wandered down to the set one day where they were filming.

Looking like a pathetic groupie, I stood next to the hoard of stargazers and watched a scene being filmed. I was even fortunate to catch a glimpse of Mr. Bridges himself. "How cool!" I thought.

Poking around the set for a couple more hours, I soon found myself striking up conversation with several security guards, the bouncer-types whose job it was to keep people like me away from the set. One of the guards informed me that the gentleman who owned the Security Company, which was hired by the film, was looking to hire some additional staff to help for the duration of the movie.

Interested, I got a hold of the security owner and told him I was ready to assist, although I didn't look anything like his fellow recruits. But since I sounded ambitious and was in decent shape, he offered me the job anyway.

LESSON #1: Always think of the "big picture." Instead of asking myself, "What is a college graduate doing taking a security guard job for $7.00/hr?" I told myself, "Think of the enormous opportunity to break into an exciting industry!"

After two weeks of security work, I now found myself on the "inside." And it was ironic that I was now pushing people away instead of getting pushed away. It even became my responsibility to watch Jeff Bridges' chair so no one would run off with it while we were filming on the streets downtown.

During those same two weeks, I was quickly, yet tactfully and professionally, introducing myself to all the members of the American Heart film crew. And instead of going home at the end of my shift, like the other security guards, I hung around the set and continued to watch the filming process. I also collected everything I could get my hands on, such as an extra copy of the script and the production reports and call sheets, which were passed out to the crew on a daily basis. Slowly, I began to build my own production book, even though I wasn't officially on the distribution list. That became my new textbook.

One night while working a security graveyard shift after the film crew had gone home, I decided to lock myself inside a vacated warehouse, which was serving as our stage area. Rather than sit in my car, I would guard from within to make sure no one broke into the building. Feeling bold, I turned on all the lights and stood right in the middle of the film set — alone. I gazed at the various movie cameras, the costumes, the props, the set dressing...and then I located and wandered into the art department.

In that one particular room at three o'clock in the morning, as I stared at all the sketches and drawings on the walls, it finally hit me like a bolt of lightning. I wanted to work in the movie business as an illustrator!

LESSON #2: Opportunity is always presenting itself and is more than likely staring you in the face right now. Use the resources around you and your willingness to succeed as your driving forces.

Whether you want a career as a film director, a scriptwriter, a cameraman, an editor or a production illustrator, you need to be able to motivate and push yourself to the next level. Had I not gone down to the movie set that one day and talked with the film crew, I never would have succeeded in taking advantage of a golden opportunity to get my foot in the door.

As we all know, it is extremely difficult, especially when starting out in the entertainment business, to get that first foot in the door. And why is that? Because, unfortunately, there are a lot of pretentious, "too-busy-for-you" industry types who are rarely willing to throw you a bone, particularly if they don't know you. If you don't believe me, just pick up the phone and try to get through to a particular producer, director or studio executive. I bet you can't even get past their assistants (unless you happen to know them). It's nearly impossible.

You've heard the saying, "It's who you know." That's the reality. And that's why you can't rely on others to get you work. You must find that bone on your own and throw it to yourself. If you can do that, you will succeed!

To finish my story with American Heart, a couple weeks later I was introduced to the production designer, the individual in charge of the art department. Having a few minutes of his time, I expressed my interest in art and the passion to work as an illustrator. I even went so far as to convince the security company and the transportation coordinator on the film to let me design some of their work, which is usually done by the art department. I also sketched various scenes from the American Heart script in order to prove to the production designer that I could really draw. Eventually, I gave those sketches to him a few days before the film finished. Although the designer told me my drawings lacked certain elements and I was extremely "green" in storyboarding, not to mention not having a portfolio, what truly captured the designer's interest was my extreme enthusiasm and sound determination.

My art skills may have been weak, but my heart was not. And that's the potential he saw in me. Three months later, that very same production designer called me at home asking if I was available to work as his art department coordinator and storyboard artist on Paramount Picture's, The Temp, starring Timothy Hutton, Lara Flynn Boyle and Faye Dunaway. That's when I decided to never look back.

LESSON #3: Once you get that bone, run with it. Run a long, long way.

Various artwork samples from *American Heart*

Scene from *American Heart*

Rainey waiting in his car, parked on street...

Push in, focusing on Rainey.

I believe you can take all the film classes and workshops you want. You can go to college and get your film or art degree. But what you won't receive from any classroom education is the reality of what it's like out there. That you will get once you hit the pavement and start looking for work. It's called the school of hard knocks.

I became successful in the entertainment industry because of one philosophy: never quit. And for those who want to break in, particularly in the storyboard arena, think of this book as your survival guide. My goal is to help you avoid many of the mistakes I made, by giving you every piece of advice and insider tip I can share. But that's all I can do. The rest is up to you.

That means you must be motivated, you must be ambitious and you must want to succeed more than anything. If you have those qualifications, you'll do just fine. To quote a saying: "It's not the size of the dog in the fight. It's the size of the fight in the dog."

Don't worry if there isn't a movie being filmed in your hometown. You can start somewhere else. Call the local film office in your state (each state has one). To help you find the phone number, contact the Association of Film Commissions International (ACFI) at (323)462-6092 or at their website: www.afci.org. They will have a listing of every film office worldwide.

You can also check under "Government listing" in your local telephone directory. Then once you obtain the telephone numbers, contact the film office and ask what current project is in town or what may be coming soon. Whether it's a Hollywood movie, a television special or just a commercial, a production is a production. Your goal is to get yourself on a production to start building experience.

Local universities and colleges, which usually have a film department, have many eager students making films for class. When you visit those departments, you can't help but notice the bulletin boards plastered with flyers from students looking for crewmembers to work on their film projects. Take a pencil with you and write down those numbers.

Many ad agencies, which work with various production companies producing commercials, PSA's (Public Service Announcements) and corporate videos, are also tuned into upcoming projects. Get a list of those agencies and make some phone calls. There are plenty of opportunities to grab. Find and take advantage of them to start gaining experience.

Chapter Two

WHAT ARE STORYBOARDS?

Since you are reading this book, I have to assume you're interested in pursuing a storyboard career and have a little knowledge about storyboards. In any case, it would be best to begin by discussing what storyboards are.

By definition, storyboards are a visual reference depicting a particular scene or action, usually taken from a screenplay or some other form of written story line. Similar to a comic book, storyboards are a series of individually drawn pictures which, when put together in a sequence of panels, convey a visual story.

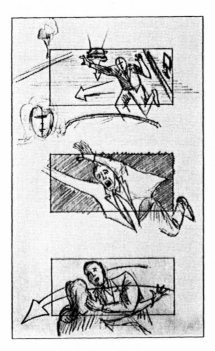

The purpose of using an artist to perform this process of storyboarding is to give the filmmaker, usually the director, a sense of how a particular scene will look before the camera rolls. This method keeps everyone from wasting time, prevents a lot of headaches, and saves the producers and production companies a lot of money. Since storyboards are usually requested for scenes containing heavy action, special effects, complex staging and difficult camerawork, other departments on the production will quickly become involved with your work, since they too will need to be educated as to what the director is trying to visually express.

12

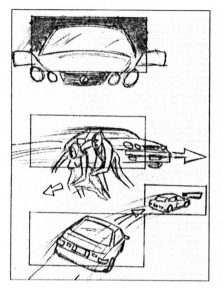

Imagine that you are a cameraman and the director is explaining to you how he or she wants a particular car chase to appear on film. Now imagine that you have not been given any visual aids to help you picture how that scene should look through the camera. Do you think you would be able to get exactly what the director has in mind on the very first take, whether for film, television or video? Storyboards help eliminate the guesswork and communication gaps when filming complex scenes.

LESSON #4: Storyboards go far beyond what you sketch on paper. They are a vital necessity for an entire production team.

When laying out a scene or sequence (discussed in more detail in the section "Teaching Yourself to Draw"), the storyboard artist will begin by meeting with the director, or whomever else the director would like in the meeting. At this time, the storyboard artist will listen and jot down notes on how particular ideas will need to be conveyed visually. After the meeting (or meetings), it is then the artist's job to convert those basic ideas into visual form for everyone to understand, hence storyboards.

The basic layout is usually three penciled panels on a 11" x 17" page, with each panel roughly 4 ½" x 9", with a brief description below each panel describing the basic action, camera angles, effects and sometimes character dialogue.

Since the sketches reflect the artist's individual style, feel free to adjust the format to your comfort level. For example, I usually put three smaller paneled sketches (1 ½" x 4") on an 8 ½" x 11" page instead of three large panels, because the directors I've worked with never gave me the luxury or time for anything else.

I also found that if I could draw less, deliver more quickly and use fewer pages, the director was much happier. I've even storyboarded sequences where I had five or six panels per page with some as small as ½" x 1 ½". You may have heard the saying, "less is more." It all depends on the director or production designer. Some may leave the layout up to you; others will request a specific format. You need to be familiar with both.

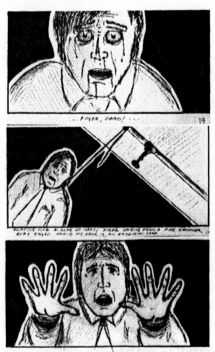

3-paneled layout vs 5-6 paneled layout

LESSON #5: Remember, the importance of storyboards is to convey the thought process visually, and to do it quickly. Focus on the scene at hand. Don't spend precious time on format, style and detail.

When you have completed your first series of storyboards, those pages will then be returned to the director for revisions and additions (another reason to draw less, it will save you time when you have to revise your boards). And finally, when the director agrees with the visual flow and presentation of your work, he or she will sign off on them, approving the storyboards for distribution. This means that they will be photocopied and handed out to the rest of the crew and production company/studio before filming the scene.

Chapter Three

EDUCATING YOURSELF

Before you begin sketching your first storyboard sequence, you still need to do more research. Like writing a book or painting a portrait, there are certain guidelines and criteria that must be applied. Don't rely on trial and error as the means for educating yourself because you'll just get frustrated and want to throw in the towel.

One of my biggest mistakes when I started storyboarding was that I didn't do enough research. If it weren't for the production designer on American Heart and The Temp as my mentor and teacher, my illustrating career would have gone right down the toilet. Because you are starting out, think of this book as your mentor and teacher.

I've always heard, "If you want to become successful, then you should study those who were successful in that particular field." I very much agree with the statement and I have found that of those who were successful, many shared a common trait. Relating to storyboards, I further discovered, after reviewing the work of many artists, that the similarities storyboard artists all possess, and which I believe make them successful, are that they clearly understand shot selection, human figure drawing and can sketch anything quickly. I believe if you can master those three elements, you too can become a successful storyboard artist.

Probably the best place to start educating yourself on what goes into a storyboard is at the local library or bookstore. The types of books you will want to get your hands on and become familiar with are those that pertain to film directing and cinematography, sketching the human figure and, of course, other books on storyboards, like this one, which contain plenty of storyboard examples.

16

Equally as important, you must understand that the director is who you ultimately will be working and sketching for. So the more you know about film directing, the more you will know what a director expects from a storyboard artist when trying to bring ideas to life.

You will also need to be educated about basic cinematography. No, this doesn't mean how to change the film or a 35mm camera lens. What it means is that you need to become familiar with various camera movements and angles and how they are achieved. Therefore, when a director tells you one day, "I want to pan to the boat, dolly in for a close-up of the captain and get an up-angle as he's knocked overboard," you will know exactly what he or she is talking about. You will also be able to sketch the sequence.

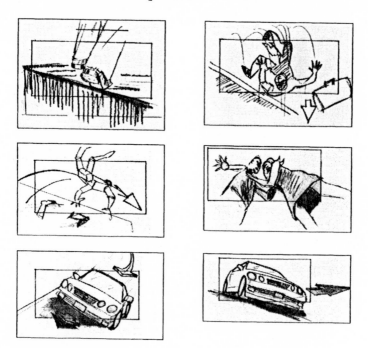

Various cinematographic angles

LESSON #6: You should always be able to think visually and sketch quickly, in any situation.

One of the best books, and one that I purchased when I began in the business, is Film Directing — Shot by Shot by Steven D. Katz. Not only does this book discuss the elements of directing, but it also contains a wealth of information on cinematography, camera movements and angles, and an excellent chapter on storyboards, along with plenty of sample storyboards. Make sure you pick up a copy of this book.

Other books worth mentioning are Film Directing —Cinematic Motion, also by Steven D. Katz, Directing 101 by Ernest Pintoff, M.F.A., and The Director's Journey by Mark W. Travis.

Another educational tool, ideal for stimulating your brain to think visually, is the comic book. Comics are an excellent and inexpensive resource for learning how to tell a story through pictures. Every illustrated panel reveals camera angle, or point of view, the character's placement and body movement, the setting, the mood, and in general, the action of the scene. Other than character dialogue, everything is exposed in a series of pictures. Storyboards, although never as detailed as comic illustrations, are very similar. In fact, you will find later that many storyboard artists you will come into contact with have done work, in one fashion or another, with comic illustration.

Comic book cover

18

Regarding educating yourself on the basics of human figure drawing, I will discuss this topic in greater detail in the section "Teaching Yourself to Draw." But, as far as books are concerned, again I believe that comic books are the best and most easily attainable resource to study. They are chock-full of illustrations of the human figure in all forms of motion and expression, and they always seem to be drawn from a unique angle or point of view. Comics are truly an inexpensive way of educating yourself. Do yourself a favor and pick up a stack of them for your reference library.

Finally, going to the movies, watching television, particularly made-for-television movies, and studying commercials (the best of them air during the Super Bowl) are also a form of education.

After the director has reviewed your storyboards, passed them onto the crew as a visual guide, and everyone's interpretation of the scene or sequence is solidified, the cameras are allowed to roll. The result after months of filming and post-production is the finished product that you see in either the theatre or on television.

The next time you're watching a movie or kicking back in front of the tube, pay particularly close attention to the various camera movements and angles that are used, along with the staging of the actors, the over-all mood and the action of the scene. Also visualize how that particu-lar scene or sequence would have looked if it were sketched on paper. How would you have storyboarded the sequence? How many panels would it have taken you to storyboard the event? Would you have used a better camera angle or lighting technique to improve a particular shot? These are questions a serious storyboard artist should ask, because the better you are at thinking visually, the better and more successful you will become.

Chapter Four

GIVING YOUR ALL

Let's summarize what we have learned so far:

- There are resources and opportunities all around you. Keep your eyes open to them, and use them.
- A storyboard is a visual reference that depicts a particular scene or action, usually taken from a screenplay or other written storyline. It consists of a series of individually drawn pictures which, put together, convey a visual story.
- Read all you can about storyboarding and film directing; study people who are successful in the field; understand shot selection and human figure drawing; lean to sketch quickly.

It is very important that you give your all by spending as much time as you can learning about storyboards. Simultaneously, you should always keep your eyes and ears open for any job opportunities that suddenly arise. You've heard the saying, "Timing is everything." Look at what American Heart did for me. The last thing you want is to be researching and reading all that you can about storyboards while being oblivious to a production crew that's in your town filming a movie. Try to do both — educate yourself and stay in tune with what's going on in your area.

Let me give you one more piece of advice on getting yourself going. Whenever you meet someone in the entertainment industry, a fellow storyboard artist, an ad agency representative or someone from your local film commission, always make sure you write down their names, their phone numbers, and what they do. Meeting and making contacts is extremely helpful to your career. The more contacts you have in your address book, the greater the chances that you will get work as a storyboard artist.

PART II
STORYBOARD TECHNIQUE

Chapter Five

STORYBOARD DEMAND

Before we get into the fundamentals of drawing, I would like to briefly revisit the importance of storyboards. This topic is extremely critical to your career as an illustrator because the more you understand how important storyboards are, the better you will be able to draw them and the greater the demand will be for your work. After all, isn't one of your objectives to become a hot commodity and be known around town as a prolific storyboard artist?

Every movie I have worked on in Hollywood has needed a storyboard artist, and one has always been hired. For example, I have worked with numerous low budget, independent production companies; the large, prominent Hollywood movie studios; and those in between.

With independent film makers, the common saying has always been, "We just don't have the budget." Those "indie" films had barely enough funding to hire a storyboard artist, so they would pay artists like me to board just the major action sequences, even though the directors always wanted about half the script to be sketched for them.

Since I refused to illustrate for free, I was usually given only two or three scenes to storyboard, resulting in about 25 to 30 pages of sketch work (using my style and format). In terms of time, individual projects like the low budget, independent films kept me employed for about two weeks. Not enough to pay the bills.

Then came a large studio picture, like "Ace Ventura: When Nature Calls" (Morgan Creek Prods. & Warner Bros.). There was a $50 million dollar movie that didn't skimp one iota, even though they'd still tell me "We just don't have the budget."

In fact, so much money was pumped into that movie, we feasted on Denver omelets for breakfast and Australian lobster tails and New York steaks for lunch. And when actor Jim Carrey and the rest of us got too hot in the sweltering summer heat of South Carolina, outdoor air-conditioning was trucked in and piped through portable cooling tents set up in the parking lots.

There were two storyboard artists hired for the film. The first artist worked during pre-production and traveled to San Antonio (the first location) sketching various storyboard sequences necessary for filming the first half of the movie. The second storyboard artist, who took over the second half of the picture in South Carolina (and who was already aboard the film as the director's assistant) was me! Being paid very healthy wages and having our four-star meals, housing and transportation paid for by the production, I enjoyed a steady stream of weekly paychecks directly deposited into my bank account.

So what is the point of all this? Well, first let me ask you a question. If you were a storyboard artist and you decided that being an illustrator was how you were going to make your living, what option would you choose? The low budget, independent route where you might make enough to pay a month's rent, or the big-budget studio films, which generally pay union rates and take very good care of you in the process?

The more time you spend learning about storyboards, reading about directing and filmmaking, and sketching and drawing, the better storyboard artist you will become. And the better the storyboard artist you become, the greater the demand for your work and the larger the movies you will be asked to work on.

Remember this the next time you feel too lazy to run down to the art store to get more paper and pencils. The bottom line is: Set your sights high. You'll be glad you did.

LESSON #7: Remember to think of the "big picture." It is an excellent motivator and will keep you from getting discouraged.

23

Chapter Six

THINKING VISUALLY

Since storyboards are, more or less, a series of drawings on a stationary sheet of paper, your goal as an artist must be to bring that paper to life. The series of storyboard pages you will create need to flow and keep up with the continuity and action of the scene. This means there must be movement in your storyboards, which is really the movement of the camera. In other words, every panel of your storyboard represents a particular frame as seen through the camera's point of view. Let's discuss this further.

Beginning with the border of your first frame, think of the box you have drawn as the eye of the camera. Everything inside the box is what the camera sees. Everything outside is not. That's why it's necessary to draw your borders with a specific format in mind. For example, in television, the framed border is usually square. In film, a rectangular cinematic border is commonly used.

35mm Film, Storyboard Frame	Television, Storyboard Frame

There are two basic approaches to drawing these borders. Some artists will sketch first, then frame the drawing later with the appropriate border. The second approach, which I find much easier and much more efficient, is to use a pre-drawn template. What I like to do is draw three correctly proportioned borders centered on a standard 8 ½" x 11" sheet of white bond paper, creating the "template." Then I produce an ample supply of nice, clean copies from my original to draw on later.

24

I use this timesaving technique because when I am in meetings with the director or am requested to hammer out a quick storyboard sequence, I can grab a stack of my pre-drawn borders and immediately begin sketching. This eliminates the worry of drawing something too large or small or taking the time to frame everything at the end.

Remember, one of the keys to becoming a successful storyboard artist is to sketch and deliver quickly. Why not start out by being one step ahead?

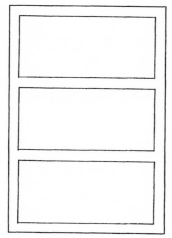

Sample 3-panel storyboard template

After your borders have been properly positioned on the page, it's time to start thinking about the camera's point of view. Remembering that storyboards reflect movement and action, you first must decide what camera angles you will want to use and how the particular scene will develop and feel using the camera lens. Let me help you understand this theory by illustrating the concept through a detailed example.

The director has handed you a couple pages from a screenplay. Your job now is to storyboard the particular scene so the director and his team can discuss the filming prior to the scheduled shoot date. The scene reads as follows:

EXT. MOVIE THEATRE, MAIN STREET – AFTERNOON

A statuesque brick building on this sleepy little street in this sleepy little mid-Western town. It's cold out. As people stroll by we can see their breath.

A fat-tired bicycle rests against glass cases advertising coming attractions. Now playing: "OLD MAN AND THE SEA."

Suddenly, the front door of the theatre BURSTS OPEN and MILTON WHITEHURST, 12, sprints outside and hops on his bike.

ANGLE

At the edge of town, Milton takes a sharp turn and what he sees makes him suddenly slam on his brakes—

EMILE, a kid from school. Big. Tough. Wears an oversized TOOTH on a chain around his neck. Blocking Milton's path with a bike of his own. A face-off—

> EMILE
> (ominous)
> C'mere yah little hoser.

Emile peels tape from his handlebars, and as he slowly moves toward Milton, he wraps his knuckles with it like a boxer.

> MILTON
> (standing brave)
> I'm a lover, not a fighter.

Emile nods. Then hits Milton square in the nose. One shot.
> EMILE
> Yer a hoser.

ANGLE

Clutching his bleeding nose, Milton watches Emile ride away.

> MILTON
> (to himself)
> a hoser and a lover.

26

After reading the scene, you quickly get an overall sense of what is visually transpiring in the story. A kid leaves the movie theatre, jumps on his bike, sees a bully from school, challenges him, gets punched in the nose and the scene ends with the bully riding off on his bicycle. Sounds simple enough. Now, you need to add the visual presence to the scripted words. For this, you'll need to put on your thinking cap to decide how best to draw the sequence of panels, so not only you, but also the director will get a feel for how the scene should look when filmed.

Starting from the beginning of the scene, it looks like we have an establishing shot so the audience can get a feel of the setting. There's a brick building and some people milling about in the cold weather, which is evident by their breath.

Here, you may start with an aerial shot looking down on the town, followed by a zoom in on the people walking through. On the other hand, you may want to start on the roof of the brick building, then crane down to the street, picking up the people walking by. Finally, you may want to start on the ground, look up at the building and then slowly pull back, widening the shot so the people walk right into frame.

Speaking earlier with the director about this sequence, you're informed that, due to budget constraints, there is no arrangement for aerial or helicopter photography or a crane for the opening sequence. So it looks like your first panel will begin with the camera down low looking up at the building, with the intention to widen and tilt down catching the people in action. To help get the idea across, you'll add some arrows to indicate the camera and atmosphere movement. Presto! There's the first shot on paper.

Moving forward to the next shot, you have a couple of options. You can keep the focus first on the people and then, after a beat, zoom past them and in on the bicycle and movie sign, giving a nice transition into the theatre. Or, you can move from a close-up of the people to an extreme close-up of their cold breath, having the camera dissolve into it, and then fade up to the movie sign while widening to catch the bicycle. Both options are nice, but given the simplicity of the scene, you choose the first option. You also throw in some arrows to help with camera movement.

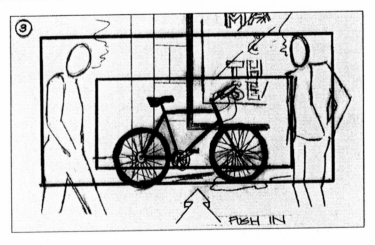

Continuing, we now have Milton running out the front door of the theatre, sprinting and jumping on his bicycle. Since this is fast-moving action, perhaps we start low with the camera as well as a close-up of the doors getting thrown open for dramatic effect, then pull back and pan, track or dolly with Milton, also using arrows, as he runs over to his bike and hops on.

And so on...

You can see the importance of the visual thought process and the need to be familiar with various camera angles, movements, and equipment as well as having insight into what the director may be visualizing.

In the first few panels, the following camera angle options were mentioned: Low angle, pan, wide-shot, zoom, close-up, track and dolly. You should really be familiar with the various angles and camera movements used. It might also be a good idea for you to get out those comic books. Flipping through the pages, you'll discover that the many angles and movements used in comics are very similar to how I use them to help me storyboard.

In addition, if you later find yourself storyboarding a sequence and know from your prior meetings with the director that there's no plan to hire a helicopter or crane, for example, for a particular sequence, then don't put it in your sketches. Instead, find out from the director and cinematographer what equipment might be used, and then sketch creatively and visually using those parameters.

Your ability to think visually will continue to get better with practice, so don't worry if you aren't familiar with all the camera angles, or you don't feel you're being very creative. Instead, educate yourself on the basics and implement them in your boards, while always making sure you're giving it your all.

Eventually, once you've worked on a handful of productions with skilled directors and camera operators, you'll pick up new and unique angles, such as camera tilts, underwater/fish-eye viewpoints and reflection shots to enhance your boards. But for right now, just learn and stick to the basics.

LESSON #8: When storyboarding a particular sequence, visualize yourself looking through the camera lens.

Chapter Seven

TEACHING YOUSELF TO DRAW

You don't have to live in a loft to be a storyboard artist. You don't have to be able to understand Picasso or Da Vinci. You don't even have to own an easel or be a member of a local art museum. What you do need is plenty of determination and discipline. You need to be able to wake up every morning and motivate yourself. You need to be willing to teach yourself the basics of drawing and have the constant craving to learn more.

Think of storyboard art and education as a peanut butter and jelly sandwich. Without both ingredients, you've got a far less interesting sandwich. And why would you want something bland and tasteless? Make that sandwich scrumptious. Make yourself a mouth-watering triple-decker. In other words, forget the textbook approach or the tiresome art classes in basic drawing. Go out there, teach yourself and get excited about wanting to learn more. Get in the trenches with your pencil and start by practicing.

I've mentioned that I started out not knowing anything about story-boards, and that I've been down that same road you are about to embark upon. In fact, I've never taken an art class or been taught how to draw. Everything I accomplished I did by teaching myself. I'm going to save you a lot of valuable time and frustration by providing you with some simple pointers on teaching yourself to draw story-boards much more quickly, easily and far better than you could have ever imagined.

HUMAN FIGURE & VISUAL REFERENCE

The most popular form of drawing, and the most difficult I found, is figure drawing, along with drawing people in various forms of motion.

31

When you begin storyboarding, whether for a production designer or director, you discover that no matter what the scene calls for or what action is taking place, people are always involved. Whether the main actor is in a fight scene or a crowd of people are in the background, people are involved. So if you're unable to draw people, your boards will turn out like that plain, boring sandwich that no one wants.

The good news is that there are several ways to quickly teach yourself how to draw people and draw them effectively.

Before I began drawing storyboards, I couldn't sketch people at all. My drawings were better than basic stick figure drawings, but far from a uniform body-type of sketch. I would find that either the people's heads I drew were three times the size of the body or one leg was two feet longer than the other; and no, I wasn't working on a monster movie where this would be deemed acceptable. So I began to teach myself how to draw the human figure properly, proportionally and how to do it fast. As you now know, speed is equally as important as conveying the visual story.

The first plan of action I embarked upon was to gather as many visual aids as I could on body composition. I started with a visit to local library, one that had an ample supply of art books.

I browsed the aisles that had books on the human body, particularly picture books. These can be found in sections which specifically pertain to the human body, or they can be found in the art section. I thumbed through those books and looked for people in various positions or forms of motion.

There was even a series of books which included virtually every angle of the human head and body for adults and children, male and female. Every possible angle that you could imagine was displayed in these books with a photograph of an actual human model — standing, turning, walking, running, sitting, bending, dressing, kicking, falling and hitting. I highly recommend you get your hands on illustrative books like these and use them as a visual reference to help you draw people.

Another great reference source is the local comic book store, where hundreds of comics line the shelves. They contain page after page of people in action. Similar to storyboards, comic books are nothing more than visual stories displayed in various pictures.

Pick up several comic books and go home and study them. Notice the different angles the artist uses. Notice the various shading, which reflects a certain mood or atmosphere the artist is trying to convey. Notice the particular expressions on the faces. Notice how the pictures tell the story, not the words. Remember your job as a storyboard artist is not to create a written story, but rather, a visual picture for everyone to understand.

LAYING OUT THE PAGE

Since we're on the topic of storyboard design, let's take a minute to understand correct storyboard layout.

When I started in the film business, the very first production designer I worked with preferred storyboards on 11"x 17" paper with three rectangle panels per page. Each rectangle was roughly 4 ½" x 9". It wasn't until after storyboarding numerous sequences that I later discovered my own style and dimensions that I found easier to use. Since time is always of the essence in storyboarding, I found that sketching three large panels per page was just too time consuming. When I worked as a storyboard artist for the Paramount film, The Temp, in 1992, I met a fellow storyboard artist who had a great approach. He was hired to storyboard complex action sequences, which required 15 to 30 pages of drawings. He would draw five to six panels per page and get them on a standard 8 ½" x 11" sheet of paper. Sometimes he would even draw a panel as small as 1" x 2".

I quickly modeled my style after his, because I liked how he laid out his panels with "time of the essence" in mind. Besides, why draw more than you have to?

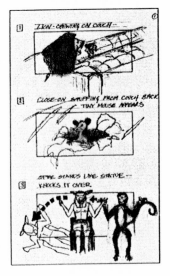

Various styles of storyboards

If you are going to be successful, I believe that you must study and compare your work to that of others in your field. Like watching tapes of Michael Jordan play basketball or a great chef preparing a tantalizing dinner, you will quickly pick up pointers if you continually watch and absorb what the professionals do.

Don't panic if you don't have the luxury of knowing any storyboard artists. Contact your local storyboard/artist union or agencies which represent storyboard artists or production illustrators. Have them send you samples of various storyboards so you can get a feel for how the finished product looks. If the agency questions you, just say that you're interested in hiring one or two of their artists and you would like to see their work.

Another great resource to help you understand storyboard layout and design is books. Yes, that's right, back to the library or bookstores. The books I have found most useful and informative are those based on popular movies. For example: Bram Stoker's Dracula, Star Wars or Raiders of the Lost Ark. All these movies have great picture books with excellent sections on storyboards.

You can even get several educational books that are full of sample storyboards for you to browse and study. One great one that comes to mind is Film Directing – Shot by Shot, published by Michael Wiese Productions. This book, which I used as a guide when learning how to draw storyboards, has plenty of sample storyboards, not to mention tips on camera angles and visualization techniques.

Stock up on plenty of these reference books and storyboard samples that you can thumb through to get a feel for how other storyboard artists create their boards. Not only will you gain valuable information, but you will also start to get an idea of how storyboards are drawn and how they all serve the purpose of telling a visual story through pictures.

FIGURE DRAWING

After thoroughly educating yourself, it's finally time to put the wheels in motion. Time to get yourself lots of blank white paper or a stack of your pre-drawn storyboard frames and preferably No. 2 pencils. Of course, don't forget the erasers. Lock yourself in a room and start practicing sketching people.

To help you get started, let's pick a body in motion from either a page in a comic book or another picture book, demonstrating a body doing something. Set that drawing next to you and study it for a minute. Next, grab your pencil and start by thinking of that human body you are looking at as if it were in four sections. You have the head, the body or torso and the arms and legs.

Now, let's start with the head by representing it on your paper as an oval. So far, so good? Next, look at the picture from the book again and add the body by representing it on your paper as a rectangle. Finally, look at your subject again and add the two arms and legs just as if you were drawing a stick figure.

Okay, now put your pencil down and look at your drawing. How does the basic shape of the body look? Is the head too big? Too small? Is the body or torso too long? Too short? How about the arms and legs? Are they bending in the right direction? Are the arms the same length? How about the legs? Once you get the basic shapes down, then you can go back and start filling in the rest. For example, to add the hands, start by drawing a little circle at the end of your stick arm representing the palm. Then add five little lines indicating the fingers and thumb. Fill in the arm and leg lines with long, narrow cylindrical shapes. Angle the rectangle of the torso by giving it a wider area in the upper body and narrower space at the waist, with a smaller rectangle indicating the hips. See, you're drawing a basic body shape in action already.

Now, keep practicing. Remember, determination and discipline are the ultimate keys to storyboard success. Keep finding new angles from your books to draw, and draw them. Start by using the simple line approach like we just did, and then go back and fill in the rest.

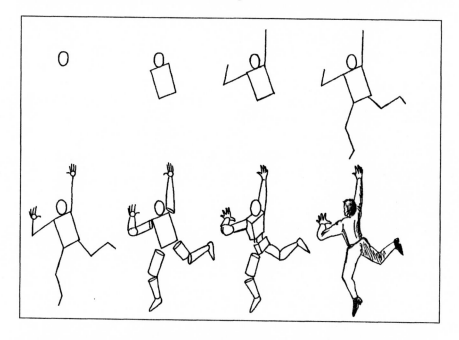

Becoming a great storyboard artist means being able to sketch anything and sketch it fast. Storyboarding isn't like a fine arts class where eyebrows and fingernails are a necessity.

A director wants to see how the scene will appear visually and what angles are best suited for the camera. He or she is not interested in whether the person you draw has any hair or forgot to put on their pants, unless those two items are of great importance to the scene. What the director wants to see is the angle of the person you drew and how the person is represented in the scene.

For instance, if the director wants to storyboard a "hit-and-run" sequence, the areas of interest in your storyboard panels are going to be the relationship of the person that gets hit to the car on the street. The director's focus will be on the action and how the person and the car interact. No one cares if your person is missing an ear or a car is missing a door handle.

The point is to spend your time learning and practicing the art of accurately drawing people — in various positions — in motion. Don't spend time on detail. That was a big mistake of mine. Save that for when you do want to become a fine artist. Until then, get the body language down and make the body uniform in shape. That means no more balloon heads or pirate legs. Once you get comfortable with drawing, you can practice speeding up the sketching process.

ADDING THE OBJECTS

Once you have sketched hundreds of various bodies in motion, it's time to put those bodies together with other objects. A child throwing food, a woman riding a bicycle, a man mowing the lawn, a grandfather pushing his wheelchair. Whatever the situation may be, the body you draw will always be in some form of motion.

A director or production designer won't hire you to draw ten pages of two people sitting on a couch talking to one another. They're hiring you to help them visualize complex scenes so they can better convey their thought process to the rest of the production crew.

The purpose of storyboards is to understand the action of a scene. Remember that.

As you know, objects are everywhere around us. The quickest way to learn how to draw objects is to choose an object to draw and then find a picture of it, just like we do with the human body. If you want to draw bicycles, get a magazine on bicycles. If you want to draw cars, get a magazine on cars.

There's virtually a magazine for everything you want to draw and magazine's are cheap and chock-full of pictures. Have access to the Internet? Surfing the "net" on a computer allows you to search for literally any object you want and within seconds find a picture of it.

The part I enjoy most about drawing objects is that they are much easier to draw than people. Why? Because objects are, for the most part, stationary. They don't twist, they don't sit, they don't run and they don't kick. If you have to draw a lawnmower or bicycle, it's a pretty straightforward task. There are usually two matching sides with a top and bottom. They don't have the multitude of angles, movements, positions and expressions that a person has. To me, that makes drawing objects easier.

To get started drawing objects, follow the same steps we used when we were drawing people. Begin with basic lines until you have the general shape on paper. Then go back and fill in those lines to add body and depth to your sketch.

If you find later that you still can't get your sketches to resemble the actual object, I have a little secret in overcoming this obstacle. What you will need is some tracing paper and a window. Forget the light table; it costs too much.

Find the picture you want to sketch and tape that picture to the windowpane so the light penetrates through. You can also use a lampshade to accomplish the same technique, especially when drawing at night. Next, grab your tracing paper and pencil and outline the object from the magazine.

When you are finished, remove the photograph, tape your tracing of the object to the window and then place a blank sheet of paper or your pre-drawn storyboard page over your tracing. Now, all that's left for you to do is trace your penciled object to your new page.

It's that easy. By the way, to answer the question, "Is this cheating?" I say, "No, it isn't." After all, didn't you just do all the pencil work yourself?

PUTTING IT ALL TOGETHER

After spending plenty of quality time sketching page after page of various objects, from frisbees to telephones, it's time to put both person and object together, with the end result being a series of storyboard panels, which will convey the action of a scene. Of course, this will come from lots of practice, determination and discipline.

Furthermore, I recommend that you make yourself a schedule, which allows you to draw at least one hour a day. This will help you get more comfortable with drawing and it will keep you from getting rusty. The last thing you want to happen is to get a call from a director or production designer when you haven't drawn anything in six months. For some reason, if you find that you can't keep to this schedule (what happened to determination and discipline?), then enroll in a basic art class, but a class in which the primary focus is on sketching and not lecturing. Then, you'll be highly motivated to sketch, because you'll be paying for the class.

Okay, time for another helpful hint in putting an action sequence together using both human figures and objects. When I was working on the movie, "Ace Ventura: When Nature Calls," the director asked me to storyboard a scene in which Ace Ventura (played by Jim Carrey) was chasing the villain in a giant monster truck through the jungle. The scene played out to where Ace ended up throwing a cigarette lighter out of his window, which landed on the villain's lap causing the villain to crash into a tree.

The problem was, I didn't know the first thing about monster trucks other than that they had really big tires. In fact, I had never seen one of those trucks up close. I had never drawn one. I'd never had the desire to draw one.

But now I was on location in South Carolina and the director was standing right in front of me asking that I storyboard the scene with the monster truck. Yikes! It obviously was my wake-up call to quickly teach myself how to draw the scene, without any time to spare.

Rather than panic, I first visualized in my head how I wanted the monster truck scene to look, just like we discussed in the chapter "Thinking Visually." I thought about the various angles I wanted to use. I thought about the close-up shots and the wide-angle shots. I thought about the mood. And, of course, I thought about the action of the scene, obviously the most important consideration.

This is another reason why I urge you to pick up several books on camera angles or enroll in a cinema class which teaches basic directing skills. It will help you open your mind and explore different ways of looking at something.

By making yourself more creative and expressive, you will add much more "punch" to your storyboards, giving your work more unique angles and movement the director may have never considered.

After a good half-hour of brainstorming the monster truck scene, I started by grabbing a stack of my pre-drawn panels. Then I wrote down inside each panel a brief description of the picture I wanted to draw. For example, Panel 1: Wide shot of monster truck chasing villain's car through bushes. Panel 2: Close-up of villain's eyes expressing fear. Panel 3: Low angle of Ace closing in.

I did this until I got to the last panel, which was the villain's car smashing into a tree. Now, all I needed was the visual reference material to draw from, just as we did when we were learning to draw human bodies and objects.

Using a friend of mine from the film set, I quickly had him get into the monster truck which sat idle in the parking lot. I had him pretend he was driving. I had his hand shifting the gear stick. I had his finger push in the cigarette lighter. I had him pretend he was throwing the lighter out the window. And the entire time he was performing all these different actions, I was taking pictures of him at various angles using my Polaroid camera.

There is always a Polaroid available on a movie set, but I highly recommend that you go out and get yourself one.

If I wanted to capture a low angle of Ace Ventura driving, I crouched down low and took a picture of my friend in the truck. If I wanted a close-up of Ace's finger pressing the cigarette lighter, I got inside the truck and snapped a shot of my friend performing that activity. The great thing about using Polaroid cameras is that you don't have to wait for the film to develop. If the picture or angle, for some reason, doesn't turn out the way I envision, I just take another. I repeat this procedure until I feel I have all the shots I need for the sequence. Then I end the quick photo shoot and go back to my drawing table to lay out the pictures.

The monster truck from *Ace Ventura: When Nature Calls*

Stepping back from the table, I smiled knowing I had already finished the sequence the director wanted. I had the various angles, from wide establishing to close-ups, and I had a series of photographs that told a visual story of the action that was taking place. Now, it was just a matter of merely transferring those still pictures onto paper.

And how did I do that? That's right. Because I had been duly diligent and spent my earlier days learning how to sketch people and objects using visual references as a guide, all that was left was sketching and adding some really big tires to the truck and my final storyboards were finished! Not bad for having never drawn a monster truck or car chase scene before!

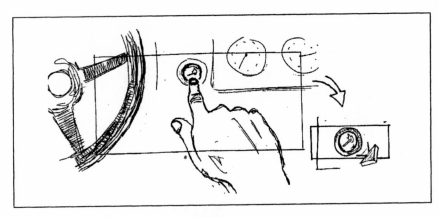

Chapter Eight

TRICKS OF THE TRADE

Many of the tricks and tips that you will discover will come by way of experience and on-the-job training. As you work in the industry, you will become familiar with what works and what doesn't. You will also learn what is more efficient, cost-effective and timesaving, and in general, what will make your life as a storyboard artist easier.

I have already shared with you a few of the "tricks" I discovered over the years. To help you remember, they are:

• **Get and use a Polaroid camera.** When you are asked to draw a particular angle, person in motion or particular object, let the camera help you. Rather than draw from memory or recall what something looked like, go out and take a picture (or pictures) of what you need and how it appears at a variety of angles. Then all you have to do is draw from the pictures. It's easier, quicker and much more accurate. You may even want to photograph an entire sequence if you're having trouble envisioning the layout.

Snapping a photo on set

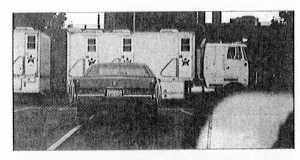

Rear of movie
vehicle in lot

Side angle

The finished storyboard
panel using my Poloroid
as visual reference

- **Use pre-drawn storyboard frames when sketching a sequence.** Get a blank 8 ½" x 11" sheet of white paper and, using a ruler and a black, fine-point permanent marker, make and center three individual storyboard frames on your page. Then take the original and make a stack of nice, clean copies. Later, when you're asked to quickly sketch a scene or put together a complex sequence, you will already be one step ahead and won't have to spend valuable time framing your work. This technique also keeps beginning storyboard artists from drawing too much on the page.

- **Smaller sketches mean quicker storyboards.** I told you there were times in my career when I was putting 5, 6, even 7 panels on a page. Since the importance of storyboards is to convey an idea, some directors will find it's more important for the production team to understand their vision than the artwork itself. This, however, does NOT mean you can produce average work and get away with it. What it does mean is that when you are pressed for time in delivering an urgently requested storyboard sequence, you will be able to put more on a page, by drawing less per panel, enabling you to get through the sequence quicker.

Now, here are a few more words of advice worth mentioning:

Cutting and pasting instead of re-drawing will save you valuable time, especially when you are revising your storyboards. Of the many storyboards you will draw, many will be revised after the director has looked at them. Another possibility is that a particular scene or sequence may be altered after you have already drawn the sequence, thus requiring that you revise it.

Using the monster truck example from Ace Ventura, originally the scene was written using two jeeps. When the monster truck was added later, the storyboards had to be revised so Ace Ventura's jeep was replaced with a monster truck. Instead of re-drawing the entire sequence, many of the storyboard pages were reusable by cutting out

Ace's jeep and pasting in a sketched version of the monster truck. After all, the switch didn't affect much of the background and surrounding scenery, so redrawing those elements would not have used my time wisely. Cutting and pasting works wonders in situations like these.

Being hired as a director's assistant is a sure-fire way of getting storyboard work. In fact, I preferred working as a director's assistant for a number of reasons. First, directors are the captains of the ships and the individuals who hire the production designer. Directors are the ones who meet with you and explain their vision. They are the people who review your storyboards and work with you to get their ideas onto paper.

Imagine working on a film with a director on a daily basis for six months, sometimes up to a year, while learning everything that goes into a production, from development to when the movie is released. Do you think you would learn about various aspects of directing and how a director works with the rest of the team? Do you think you would learn how directors use storyboards to help them direct? Do you think by being on the film set everyday and next to the camera, you would learn about camera angles and technique?

Assisting a director, in my mind, is the best job for anyone who wants to learn about movie-making and the process of how a script is transferred from written page to the screen. To a storyboard artist, that information is invaluable! Because, again, the more you can think like a director and the more you understand about camera movement and filmmaking, the better you will be as a storyboard artist.

Secondly, let's say you've read this book several times, have put together a portfolio of your work and you feel confident that you can tackle some storyboard assignments. Now imagine because of the networking you've done, you find out there's a director looking for an assistant on an upcoming movie (every director needs an assistant), so you decide to take the job, putting your portfolio aside.

What do you think will happen when that director enters pre-production and suddenly meets with the production designer to discuss hiring a storyboard artist? Surprise! That's when you proudly say, if you haven't already done so, that you are also a competent storyboard artist by trade and have a portfolio to show.

Nine times out of ten the director will hire you to also draw the storyboards because you are already his or her assistant and will be around every day through the remainder of the production. This means that you are much more convenient, dependable and cheaper then hiring another outside artist.

Of every director's assistant position I was awarded, all but one didn't have me draw the storyboards (because the one director had a son who was a storyboard artist). That one situation aside, not only did I get to draw numerous storyboards for many films, but I also learned a heck of a lot about directing and filmmaking, and my storyboards got tremendously better as a result.

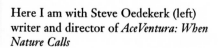

If you can't get hired as a storyboard artist, get hired as a director's assistant. You'll still find yourself storyboarding for the director.

LESSON #9: Always ask yourself "How can I make my job as a storyboard artist easier?"

Here I am with Steve Oedekerk (left) writer and director of *AceVentura: When Nature Calls*

Chapter Nine

CREATING YOUR PORTFOLIO

Before you go on your first interview, or meet with a director or production designer who will ask to see your work, you need to have a portfolio. Not only does a portfolio make you appear professional, but it is also a very organized way of presenting your storyboards and art samples, while keeping them well protected at the same time.

Unlike when I broke into the business, you should always have samples of your work to present to someone. You never know when an opportunity will arise when you get to meet with a director or production designer. When I started out, unfortunately I didn't have anything to present right off the bat, which made me look inexperienced and forced me to quickly sketch some storyboards to prove that I could actually draw.

A word of advice to you: Don't ever put yourself in that situation, because if a designer ever asks to see your work and you tell him/her you don't have anything to show, he/she won't bother meeting with you. Why? Because they figure you don't have any experience and are unprepared, and aren't ready to tackle a storyboard job. Do yourself a favor. Put together a professional looking portfolio.

More importantly, always, always, always make copies of your work. Never give anyone your original artwork. Only distribute copies. The importance of this is should you later need to update your portfolio, send samples of your work or one day write a book about your successful storyboard career, you will need your originals to make copies from. I learned this lesson the hard way.

If you don't already have a nice looking portfolio case, go and get yourself one. You can find them at any quality art store. Portfolios come in all sizes and shapes, and they range from very inexpensive to $100 or more. When I purchased mine, I bought a very large and expensive portfolio. I figured I was going to have my portfolio the rest of my life and, like a briefcase, when I walked into a meeting with a portfolio in my arm, people would see that I am a professional.

Don't think of your portfolio purchase as an expense. Think of it as an investment. Eventually, you will be putting a lot of blood, sweat and tears into your storyboards, not to mention the countless hours of sketching. So why not treat yourself and display your work in a portfolio which will make you proud. After all, it's your work.

What goes into a portfolio? In a nutshell, a portfolio should comprise samples of your best work, demonstrating a variety of drawing talent, experience and overall professionalism. As you accumulate artwork and get hired on various storyboard assignments, you will have plenty from which to choose.

Place your best work and organize it in your portfolio like a visual resume. You may also want to type small headings under the various pages explaining what assignment the particular storyboard came from and what it was used for. This way, people who peruse your portfolio can do so on their own and at their own pace. You don't have to keep looking over their shoulder saying, "Okay, now that storyboard is from..." as if you're showing them your family photo album.

You want to appear professional and as if you've been on plenty of interviews, so that you are taken seriously, which we will discuss in more detail in the chapters, "Meeting the Production Designer" and "Interviewing Do's & Don'ts."

For those who are beginning and don't have any samples to put in a portfolio, like me when I started, you need to take the time to create some. Don't worry if your samples are made up and not from any television or movie assignments. When starting out, the important thing is to prove that you can draw. The experience and list of credits will come later.

When I was on my first film, American Heart, the production designer advised me to put together a portfolio once the film was over, so I would be able to show samples of my work. I didn't have any samples so I had to create them from scratch.

First, I took some pages of the American Heart script and storyboarded a particular scene. Although they were never used on the film, it proved that I could storyboard a scene from a screenplay. Those were the first drawings in my portfolio. Then, wanting to show that I could also perform production illustration, such as background sketches, architectural renderings, figure drawing and colored-pencil work, I purchased a few of those good "step-by-step" books that teach beginners how to draw the above-mentioned items. After a good two months of work and feeling comfortable with pencil in hand, I had a portfolio that was ready for directors and production designers to see.

LESSON #10: If you want to be treated as a professional, you must think and act professionally.

Pencil sketch of barn using a step-by-step "how-to" book

Architectual rendering using an original blueprint

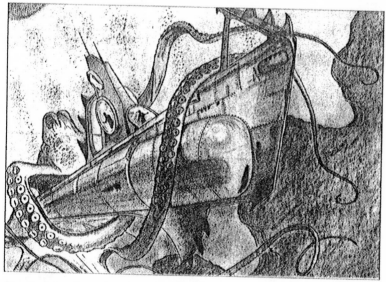

Detailed drawing using an illustration from Jules Verne's *10,000 Leagues Under The Sea*

As we did at the end of Part I, let's summarize what we've learned in this section on storyboard technique:

- The more time you spend learning about storyboards, reading about directing and filmmaking, and sketching and drawing, the better storyboard artist you will become.
- Learn to define your format and configure your camera angles. Visualize yourself looking through the camera lens. The purpose of a storyboard is to understand the action of a scene.
- For storyboarding, you don't need textbooks and classes in the art of drawing. Get in the trenches with your pencil, and start to draw. Your job is to create a visual picture for everyone to understand.
- Continue to educate yourself on the basics. Take advantage of resources —books, magazines, comic books. Study others in your field; contact agencies can be helpful.
- Practice sketching people in motion; continually search for new angles to draw from. Practice drawing objects. Finally, draw them together.
- Practice drawing at least one hour a day. If you're not disciplined to do this alone, take a class. Think "outside the box." Open your mind to new ideas. Learn "tricks of the trade" and use them!
- Create a portfolio. If you haven't worked yet, create a portfolio that shows you can draw. If you've worked in the industry, organize your best work.
- If you want to be treated as a professional, you must think and act professionally.

PART III

STORYBOARDS IN ACTION!

Chapter Ten

MEETING THE PRODUCTION DESIGNER

You've educated yourself, spent diligent hours learning how to draw, and you've put together what you think is a professional portfolio representing your best work. Now, the real test comes, sitting down for the first time to meet with a production designer, the talented individual who has been hired by the director to create the artistic look of the picture.

On big-budget films, there will usually be a production designer as well as an art director who will work together to produce the artistic design. Otherwise, there will be only the designer and his or her staff.

The production designer will decide if you have enough experience to tackle a storyboard job, so here's a piece of sound advice. It is to your best advantage to impress the hell out of them, both with what you've drawn and what you have to say. After all, it will take a considerable amount of time and patience to set up the interview in the first place. The last thing you want to do is not take full advantage of the opportunity.

After my first film experience (American Heart) was over, and I had a fresh portfolio under my arm, I set up a meeting with the production designer who was working on the television series, Northern Exposure, shooting in my home town in the state of Washington. I figured, since I was working toward a career as a storyboard artist, now was the best time to put my plan into action and show off my abilities.

I recall sitting in the art department of Northern Exposure, while learning three important points: (1) Many of the production designers in the industry know each other. (2) My portfolio was very "green," reflecting my beginning artwork. (3) I didn't have the drafting or model-making experience which the production designer really needed. The designer admitted he was a bit leery of bringing me aboard because of my lack of experience. He told me my résumé would be kept on file. In other words, he wasn't ready to hire a rookie for an enormously popular television program. I left his office extremely disappointed.

After the meeting, I took a good, long look in the mirror and told myself I wouldn't give up. I knew that breaking into the business wasn't going to be easy, and I knew I wasn't going to be hired on every interview I got. I also had to keep telling myself that there was a production designer out there, somewhere, who would discover my energy, my willingness to work hard and my refusal to quit, despite being a beginner. There had to be one designer out there who was going to hire me for my potential and not solely based on my experience. After all, every artist had to start somewhere. Fortunately, the production designer who turned out to be "the one" was Mr. Joel Schiller, the designer I had met while working on American Heart.

After American Heart had finished, Joel was hired as a production designer on director Tom Holland's Paramount film, The Temp. Joel was in the process of staffing his art department, so he contacted me at home and offered me a job as his art department coordinator and illustrator. Of course, I was ecstatic about the telephone call and accepted the offer, even though it wasn't solely a storyboard position.

While working on The Temp in Portland, Oregon, for a solid four months (with 6-day workweeks), the incredible amount of information I learned from Joel was invaluable. Not only was I now part of a film crew and had a clear understanding of how a film was made, but I was also able to work with an incredibly talented staff, including a Portland-based storyboard artist whom Joel and Tom had hired to assist since I was the rookie.

Joel also coached me on how to draw professional production illustrations, which Tom Holland used on the film to envision how certain camera shots would appear on screen. I was taught how to produce conceptual drawings for the director, and I learned how to draft and construct various scaled models needed for the filmmaking process.

Since I also had a business degree, I was put in charge of the art department purchases and petty cash account, and I was allowed to attend many of the meetings involving the storyboard artist, the director and the producers. Unfortunately, the experience also made me privy to the firing of a talented set designer in the art department because that person's work had taken too long to produce. Remember what I told you about being fast?

After The Temp finished production, I now had a revised portfolio packed with real movie-making samples, great references which I needed for future work, and a solid film under my belt.

I received my first film credit at the end of the movie, and Joel even changed my credit to read Production Illustrator, enabling me to qualify as a union storyboard artist and get into the associated union. My life as a storyboard artist catapulted after that.

A conceptual drawing at a psychiatrist's office, *The Temp*

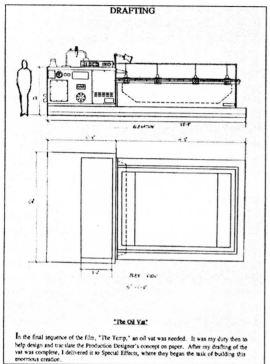

DRAFTING

"The Oil Vat"

In the final sequence of the film, "The Temp," an oil vat was needed. It was my duty then to help design and translate the Production Designer's concept on paper. After my drafting of the vat was complete, I delivered it to Special Effects, where they began the task of building this enormous creation.

Sample of drafting a giant oil vat, *The Temp*

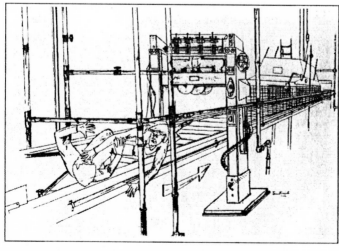

Detailed rendering of a giant mechanical dough cutter used in, *The Temp*

Production designers, like the directors, are going to be your employers, your mentors and your references. They are the people who will teach you what you need to know and what they look for when hiring. Once you work for them, it will be your job, each and every day, to learn as much as you possibly can and to ask many questions, without coming across as bothersome. They are a wealth of information.

Can you imagine what would have happened if I had met with the production designer of Northern Exposure AFTER my experience on The Temp? I can't say for certain that I would have been hired, but when asked if I had experience, the interview would have taken a completely different turn. I now had a bunch of storyboard, illustrative, drafting and model samples from a big-budget Paramount film, proving I wasn't so "green" anymore.

The point I want to stress again about production designers is to learn from them. They, more than likely, have been in the entertainment business for a very long time, and they are usually willing to help you get started. They are also the talented individuals and teachers who will, one day, down the road, hire you again.

Never pass up a job from qualified production designers when starting out. That would be one of the biggest mistakes you can make.

Begin by meeting and forming a business relationship with them, whether it's through an interview or working with them on a project. I am grateful to Joel Schiller who gave me the chance to prove myself. I hope there are more like him in the business today who are willing to help beginners. If so, you're in luck.

LESSON #11: Don't panic if you don't get hired after an interview. Learn from your meeting, and prepare for the next one.

Chapter Eleven

THE ART DEPARTMENT

Working as a storyboard artist, you will find that much of your time will be spent working at a table drawing your boards while racing against the clock. When you are not attending meetings with the director or production designer at their location, usually a production office which is set up to conduct business while a television or film project is being filmed, you will be working from home.

No, this does not mean sketching a series of storyboards on your coffee table with your feet up while watching re-runs of "I Love Lucy" or your favorite soap opera. Whoever has hired you has probably given you a good rate and, in turn, expects nothing but the best. That means you must be focused and ready to deliver your best possible work, even and especially if it's your first job.

The best environment to work in at home is an area set up to be a little "art department". This can be either in a corner of your bedroom, in the garage or basement, or better yet, in a spare or empty room. You will need plenty of good, strong lighting, as well as the following items:
- A sturdy table, preferably one with some drawers for your research material and art supplies
- A comfortable chair with good back support
- Plenty of number #2 pencils, gum erasers, rulers, charcoal (for shading), colored pencils and pens (just in case), scissors, glue-sticks, liquid paper and clear tape (for cutting and pasting)
- Your Polaroid camera and plenty of film
- A stack of your pre-drawn storyboard templates

As a side note, you should familiarize yourself with where the nearest copy machine is located, as well as the nearest fax machine. It's amazing how often you will find yourself running out the door to make copies or faxing your latest storyboards to the director and production designer, who have phoned you and are waiting anxiously for delivery.

The more you work in the storyboard industry and the more successful you become, the larger your art department will grow. In fact, I've seen workspaces at home complete with copy machines, light tables, faxes, scanners and computers. Don't worry, your time will come.

There are also times, when you may not have the luxury of working out of your house. For instance, if you become a director's assistant/storyboard artist and have to travel with the crew to film on location, you will find yourself drawing storyboards while on the set. And, let me tell you, drawing on the set is one of the worst ways to draw as far as productive work environments are concerned.

Having been a director's assistant on a handful of major studio movies, I can report that I've had to share a private trailer with the director. Most trailers consist of a couch, a kitchen table, a bed, a bathroom, a television and VCR and some counter space (this varies depending on the profile of the director). The reason I'm pointing out the specific trailer amenities is that the trailer is the only space you will be given to set up your mini-"art department," and it's important to do so without cluttering the trailer or upsetting the director.

On Ace Ventura: When Nature Calls, I spent many hours drawing at the trailer's kitchen table. I also assembled a tackle box containing my art supplies to keep with me at all times. Then, when I finished boarding a particular sequence, I would run over to the production trailer, occupied by the assistant directors and production assistants, and where a copy machine was usually available to make copies of my storyboards. Yes, the entire process was crude and impractical, but it worked. The director and department heads aren't concerned about ruler lines or toner smudges, because their main focus is on the action and how the scene is visually conveyed on paper. But cleaner copies are always nicer.

Since many of your storyboard meetings will involve the production designer, let me provide you with a brief orientation on what to expect in an actual art department during the production of a film or made-for-television movie. This will be important for you to know in order to help you get comfortable at your first meeting.

The head of the art department is the production designer, hired by the director and responsible for the artistic look of the picture. In some cases, when there is no production designer, the department head will be the art director. In other cases, the designer and art director may work together.

The rest of the staff depends on the budget, size and scope of the project. Generally speaking, there are usually one or two set designers or drafts people (architects) who are hired by the production designer or art director to draw detailed construction plans for film sets that need to be constructed. There may be model makers, scenic artists, animators and puppeteers, although those highly-specialized craftspeople usually work out of their own facility or trailer rather then inside the art department.

The art department coordinator is responsible for a number of tasks, depending on his/her experience. In my case, since my focus was on storyboards and drawing, a good portion of my time was actually spent drawing for the production designer and director. Coordinators work closely with the designer and pretty much do whatever they are told — purchase needed art supplies, control the petty cash, hunt down local vendors, drive the designer to the film set, answer phones, and work as a general liaison between the designer and any fellow workers.

Last but not least, production assistants and internship students frequent the department. They want to break into the business, and are either working for peanuts or are still enrolled in school. Productions gratefully welcome PA's and interns because: PA's are really inexpensive to hire, and interns don't get paid; both do whatever they are told; and both are usually assigned the lousy jobs no one else wants to do, such as pick up lunch, make copies and run miscellaneous errands.

For your information, many people who currently work in the entertainment industry have been production assistants and interns at one point or another in their careers. I've been a PA and intern too. For more in-depth coverage regarding the value of internships, refer to the section, "The Secrets About Internships."

There you have it the art department in a nutshell. And one is always needed, whether it's a little corner at home, or a full-blown department on a studio film. Remember, as a storyboard artist, you need to have a functional area where you can focus on your work and do the best job you can. You don't want to waste time running around the house looking for that last bottle of liquid paper or a spare roll of scotch tape. Set up an area, regardless of where it is, as long as it has sufficient light, a solid surface to draw on, a comfortable chair and a place where you can keep your art supplies in order. Delivering the best storyboards you can is your number-one goal.

LESSON #12: You never know where you will be drawing. Make sure all of your art supplies are kept together and are easily transportable.

Chapter Twelve

YOUR FIRST STORYBOARD JOB

Your first storyboard job is the most critical. That's where you will demonstrate to the director, production designer, producers and the rest of the crew what you can do. It will be your opportunity to prove to them that you understand what is needed, that you're able to meet the fast turnaround times and deadlines and, most import, that you are able to convey the director's vision on paper, that you can visually present the action of a scene so everyone can clearly understand it. If you can successfully accomplish these tasks, you shouldn't have any problem finding work.

Being able to alter your drawing style to suit a particular director or production designer is another skill you need to acquire. Some will ask for more detail in your storyboards; others will ask for less. When I was hired as the storyboard artist on Warm Texas Rain, a large independent film, the director told me, after I had delivered the first set of boards, that my work was too detailed for him, even though I had no problem meeting the deadline.

Realizing that the director was striving for a certain look, I altered my style and gave him less detail on the second series of storyboards. Being able to adapt and work with directors and production designers to give them what they want, no matter how happy you might be with your own work, is an essential part of storyboarding.

Getting back to your first storyboard assignment, whether you have been hired strictly as a freelance artist, or as a director's assistant, your primary goal on your first job is to impress the director and production designer. This doesn't mean you should be a "brown-noser" and offer to constantly shine their shoes throughout the day. What it means is, prove to them that you are professional, courteous, friendly and, above all, hard-working. Prove that you can take the bone and run with it.

When you sit down for the very first time to sketch your first set of storyboards, the first item on your agenda should be to review all your notes from prior meetings with the director and production designer. Make sure you clearly understand the scene you will be sketching and the specific action the director wants conveyed on paper. Never make the mistake of drawing something the director didn't ask for. Again, your job as the storyboard artist is to convey the director's vision — not yours. Save yours for when you become the director.

Once you've read through your notes, now is the time to lay out the scene. Pull out a stack of your storyboard templates and softly write in each panel the camera angle and action you want to draw. Continue this process until you have the entire sequence written out and you feel you have captured the idea the director has asked for. Then using your Polaroid camera, your research material, and this book, begin to storyboard the sequence in its entirety. When you have finished, look over your work and incorporate the following into your drawings:

- **Number each storyboard panel.** Each number should preferably appear in the upper left-hand corner of the frame. The number should also be circled for easy identification.

- **Briefly describe in each panel the action taking place.** Using three or four lines, indicate what you have drawn on the right-hand side, above or below the storyboard frame. You should also include the camera angle used and the corresponding scene number from the shooting script (if a film or television screenplay), so the director and crew understand what scene you have drawn.

- **To help convey the visual thought process, use arrows.** For example, if you have sketched two gunmen racing across the roof of a building, put in an arrow showing the direction the men are traveling. If a police helicopter suddenly appears from behind the building, use an arrow to help indicate the flight path of the helicopter. Eliminating the guesswork by using arrows will help to convey the action, making your storyboards easier to understand.

- **Number each storyboard page.** Do so by adding the page number on the top-right corner of the page. Should an intern happen to drop your faxed pages, he or she will be able to put the pages in order and deliver your boards to the director.

- **On the last page, at the bottom of your last storyboard panel, clearly print your full name.** When your finished boards are distributed and faxed to the crew and around town, it's like handing out your business card. You're trying to gain recognition and a name for yourself. This is an easy way to accomplish this task.

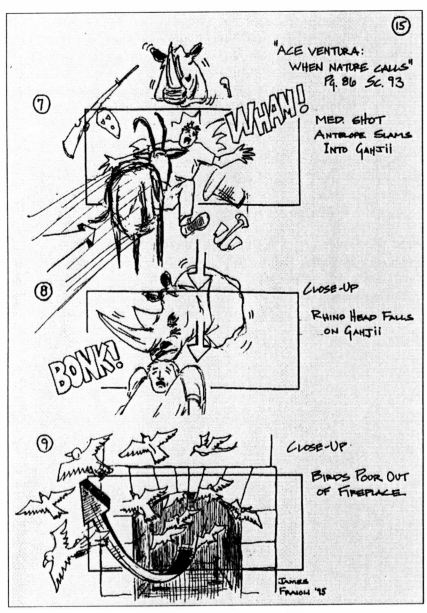

Completed storyboard page, *Ace Venture: When Nature Calls*

Finally, before you put down your pencil, do another review and check of your boards. Are you happy with your work? Do you feel the action is clearly demonstrated on your paper? Did you draw what the director or production designer asked for? Are your pages neat, clean, clear and professional looking? If you have a coffee stain on one of the pages, it might be in your best interest to re-do that page.

Once you are happy with your work, it's time to deliver. This is usually done by means of fax, in person or via a delivery or courier service. It's always tense waiting to hear what the director or designer has to say about your work, especially if you aren't working at their side as an assistant. I can't tell you how many times I've walked around the house wondering why the director or designer hasn't called me. But in the end, they always do call and they always have me illustrate their next set of boards.

Just remember to be ready to adapt to the changes you are asked to make. "Yes, that won't be a problem," are words you need to say gracefully in the entertainment business. You'll find yourself better off if you do.

LESSON #13: When starting out, be flexible and roll with the punches. If you keep your guard up and can not accept criticism of your storyboards, you will not succeed.

Chapter Thirteen

DON'T FORGET TO PLAN AHEAD

Unlike the old studio systems of years past, there are no longer permanent, full-time art positions for storyboard artists and illustrators. The days of drawing Bambi and Mickey Mouse are over. You are now considered a "work for hire" — also known as a freelancer.

Basically, you are hired for your storyboard talent, and when your services are no longer requested, you are taken off the payroll. I'm sure you've heard the expression, "It's feast or famine." For a freelancer, it's a tough way to make a living if you're having difficulty finding work. Another way to put it is that you will be making lots of money when you work, collecting unemployment when you're not, and constantly looking for your next project.

To succeed as a freelancer when starting your storyboarding career, not only do you have to be a decent storyboard artist, but you also have to be a hustler, a go-getter, and an individual with plenty of motivation. If not, you will find yourself without work for a long time.

When you have been hired, and especially when you are working on your first storyboard job, you need to be thinking in two different directions during the course of your employment. The first is to draw and deliver the best storyboards you can. The second is to develop and use your networking skills. This means introducing and "pitching" yourself to the key players in charge of the particular project you are working on.

Whether the project is a commercial, television program or feature film, the key players are generally the director, the producers, the production designer and the executives from a studio or production company (who control the money). They are also the various individuals who have the authority to hire and fire you. It's in your best interest to know who your bosses are.

We will discuss this more, but let me briefly touch on a couple of important items as you begin to prepare yourself for the freelance world.

Many of the other production people you will be working with on a particular assignment are also freelancers, like yourself. When a specific project ends, they too will need to find their next paying job. It is at this point in time when everyone seems to come together to discuss upcoming work, who's hiring, and what the next project in town is. Working with a large and very talented pool of crewmembers, you will discover that many of them will have plenty of names, phone numbers and leads to pass on to you. In fact, those who've been in the industry for some time can probably tell you the next project they will be working on.

As you get hired on various storyboard assignments, always, always, always write down the names and telephone numbers of as many of the key players and crewmembers as you can for future reference, and always keep a copy of the "Final Crew List" from each project. Also, write down the names of the future projects that the other crewmembers might have mentioned, so you can research them to find out who the director and production designers are.

The best resources for specific information about a film/TV project are The Hollywood Reporter and Daily Variety magazines. In Hollywood, they are referred to as "the trades," and they list every independent and major studio film/TV project along with the key personnel attached. They also furnish addresses and phone numbers so you can contact them. These magazines can be found at any large magazine stand or bookstore that carries entertainment literature.

You can also find information about the trades on the Internet. Better yet, make the investment and get yourself a year subscription, preferably to The Hollywood Reporter. It will keep you abreast of every project heading to your area and what's going on in the entertainment industry. It is published on a daily basis like a newspaper.

Okay, it's time for a brief scenario. Let's say, after your first storyboard assignment has ended, you suddenly find yourself without your next job lined up (remember, you're new at this and it's going to be tough in the beginning). Rather than get discouraged, now is the perfect time to update your portfolio and send letters to the key players you have just worked with, thanking them for the opportunity and looking forward to working with them again. You should also include your business card. Get some printed. They are very professional and it eliminates the need for a production designer to search for your phone number. Send a couple of copies of your best storyboards as samples (to refresh their memories). During this down time, also contact your local film commission and introduce yourself. Many of the film offices keep active files on local crewmembers for those times when out-of-town production companies need assistance in town. Make sure you send a copy of your latest resume to the film office.

October 15, 1991

Dear Joel,

Thank you for your help in getting me started in an art career in the movie business. I didn't get a chance to thank you and say good-bye, but I really enjoyed meeting and working with you.

Since the film is over, I can now concentrate on studying the sample storyboards you gave me and grasp the concepts behind the sketches. It will be very exciting now to re-read the script with storyboards in mind, and begin illustrating how I envision particular scenes. I feel very confident that my work will prove I have the talent for an art position in the film industry. By using the techniques you have taught me, I will develop a portfolio filled with storyboards and sketches you will be proud of. I understand it will take many years to master storyboards, but I have the desire and determination to reach my dream.

I am now taking time off to concentrate on my portfolio and will have it completed by the end of November. I will also let you know from time to time how everything is going. About making arrangements for coming down in December, I will call you in several weeks to confirm my travel plans. I will be staying for one week so I can hang around the studio, like you mentioned, to learn more about the art department.

Thank you again for all your help, and your interest in me as a storyboard artist. I will be keeping in touch.

Sincerely,

James O. Fraioli

4006 Hunts Point Road • Bellevue, Washington 98004 • (206) 455-4622

My thank you letter to
Joel, who hired me on
his next movie, *The Temp*

JAMES
FRAIOLI
PRODUCTION
ILLUSTRATOR

4006 Hunts Point Road
Bellevue, WA 98004
206/455/4622

My business card when starting out

77

HAPPY NEW YEAR . . .

. . . From an "AMERICAN HEART" Crew Member !

Since working on the set of "American Heart" as a security guard, as well as designing the "Film Crew" cards, I have been pursuing my career as a production illustrator. I plan to specialize in drawing storyboards.

I have met many people who have taken an interest in my work, including an art director who has invited me to Los Angeles to see my illustrations.

I do hope we can work together again in the near future. Should you need a storyboard artist or any artistic talent, please contact me.

HAPPY NEW YEAR!

James O. Fraioli

4006 Hunts Point Road. Bellevue, WA. 98004
(206) 455-4622

Here's a fun, creative way of staying in touch and reminding those of what you do

Every state also has a local film/media-index book. This is another resource that out-of-state production companies use when getting ready to staff a project. Since it is very expensive for companies to bring an entire crew on location, many of them wait until they arrive, then call the film office and thumb through the local media book to search for crewmembers. Don't let them pass you by. Contact the film commission and find out how to obtain a copy of the media book so you can get your name listed.

I went one step further. Not only did I add my name, but I included a sample drawing and a brief description of my abilities, like an advertisement. It cost a bit more than just my name, but it was well worth it. I received a lot of work from that one little ad.

You should also get your hands on a copy of the Los Angeles media book, titled, LA 411. It's a great resource to have when networking.

Storyboard artists [continued]

James O. Fraioli
206-455-4622
4006 Hunts Point Rd / Bellevue, WA 98004; Select a professional and experienced storyboard artist. The polished storyboards of James Fraioli blend imagination with artistic talent to convey the relation between word and image. Working with well-known art directors, James has clearly illuminated the complex creative process, proving that ideas can turn into reality. Portfolio and references available. **(See ad this page)**

Jaz & Jaz,
The Artist's Representative   206-282-8558

Dennis Ochsner
206-464-4833   Rep 206-447-1600
401 2nd Ave S #311 / Seattle, WA 98104; fax 206-292-8206; Dennis Ochsner, Pat Hackett, Artist Rep; Great storyboards help your concepts sell themselves. With 28 years experience as an art director and designer. I know how to translate your ideas into expressive boards. Also do ad comps, concept boards, and design comps and am willing to work at your office. **(See ad on page 69)**

Budgeting

J. Daniel Dusek
206-747-3250   L.A. 213-850-1138
1847 153rd Ave SE / Bellevue, WA 98007; **(See ad on page 77)**

David Newsom
206-631-5771
12022 SE 280th St / Kent, WA 98031; David Newsom; Ten years experience in Northwest commercial and corporate production. Script breakdowns, AICP estimating, production scheduling and job actuals analysis. Pre-production to post completion, on-time and on-budget. Professional, honest, reliable and flexible with all types of clients and sizes of projects. Northwest Ford Dealers, Weyerhaeuser, Huffy Bikes, McDonald's, Nordstrom, Leningrad Isballet. **(See ad on page 81)**

Northwest Production Consortium   ●
800-241-2113
200 W Jackson St / Medford, OR 97501; Full Circle Communications 800-241-2113. Howard Screiber; OMPA, SOFVA; Film and video production, all formats. Production management, directing, scheduling, budgeting, location scouting, 2nd unit photography, post production supervision. Camera, grip, and lighting packages. **(See ad on page 19)**

Directors

Archangel Enterprises   206-736-8575

Bennett/Watt Enterprises, Inc.
206-746-9448   800-327-2893
13410 SE 32nd / Bellevue, WA 98005; fax 206-746-7806; Jim & Kelly Watt; IA/NABET; 30 years experience in all phases of entertainment, corporate and documentary production in more than 25 countries. Clients: NBC, ABC, CBS, PBS, NHK. Call Jim Watt if you value talent, intelligence, resourcefulness, speed, great pictures and sound. TV series: "Fly Fishing Video Magazine" and "The American Frontier," starring Merlin Olsen and Charlie Jones. **(See ad on page 102)**

Brad Boiling
206-682-5417
111 S Lander St #301 / Seattle, WA 98134; fax 206-682-3038; White Rain Films; **(See ad on page 25)**

Jerry Carlton
208-384-5675
PO Box 724 / Coeur D'Alene, ID 83814; fax 208-384-5675; OK! So I've only directed student films and the smallest theatre production company in Europe, but I'm anxious to take your feature, commercial or industrial and direct it. Or, I'm a versatile production ramrod, 1st or 2nd Assistant Director. I know Idaho. I love film. I'm ready. **(See ad on page 86)**

JAMES
FRAIOLI
SKETCHING
ILLUSTRATIONS
STORYBOARDS
206-455-4622

My advertisement in the local media book

Local media and advertising newspapers are also great for placing an inexpensive ad. They get your name out there.

Sample industry newspaper ad

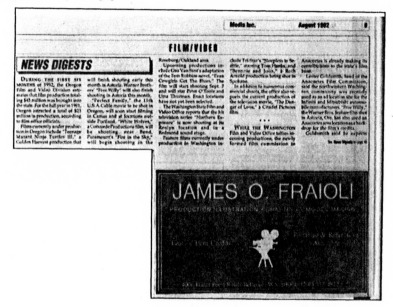

Still have too much free time on your hands? Surf the web and place online Internet ads for yourself. Heck, maybe even create your own personal website. Yes, most important is your ability to deliver great storyboards, but you need to market yourself and be your own P.R. person. The more you advertise, the more letters you write to stay in contact with fellow crewmembers, and the more names and numbers you obtain — the more opportunities you may create for yourself when needing to find work.

It's going to be a rough road to the top, and you may feel as if you're constantly fighting an uphill battle, but believe me, the more you network and the more you plan ahead, the more your telephone will ring and the easier it will be to find work. Remember, never give up!

LESSON #14: Don't wait until the last day to ask about upcoming or future work. Start as soon as you're hired.

Chapter fourteen

GETTING PAID vs WORKING FREE

You've finally received the phone call you've been waiting for. Someone wants you to be their storyboard artist for an upcoming film. Let's say you hear that your name came from a crewmember you worked with previously or from an ad you placed in the local media book. And the film company is ready to go! They have a production office, a script, and a huge request for storyboards.

What they don't tell you is that they want you to storyboard free. A polite and sneaky way of saying this is, "They want you to work deferred." Then they quickly promise you the moon. They tell you that once they obtain financing for the movie, you will be paid your storyboard rate. They may even promise you back-end points too, giving you the chance to make even more money should the movie get sold to a distributor. And so on, and so on....

In other words, what they are asking you to do is storyboard their script free of charge because they don't have any money to pay you, and they need your drawings to help pitch their idea to possible investors. Do you take the job?

Let me give you another scenario. A production designer calls you from out-of-state. He says he got your name and resume from a letter you had sent him two months ago inquiring about work. He tells you the film he is working on has a very small budget, but it's a Warner Brothers film, to be released in theaters the following year. Because of budget constraints, he wants to hire you as his coordinator, but can't pay you the industry rate. Instead, he offers you very little money and asks if you are willing to work as a local hire, meaning that you have to pay to get yourself to the state in which they are filming, house yourself, and fork out any other additional costs required. Do you take the job?

Getting paid versus working free is like the difference between a golden opportunity and a scam. There's a fine line that separates them. There are those who will try and bait you in order to save a dollar, and there are those who will see your potential and offer you a chance to prove yourself. The toughest part lies in being able to distinguish the scam artists from the legitimate players. This ability comes only with experience, and probably after you've been burned a couple of times.

During my career as a storyboard artist, I received many calls for storyboard work, from those who were willing to pay me, and those who wanted me to draw for free. My simple rule in the beginning was, if I had heard of the people who were calling and the project provided me with additional experience and better samples for my portfolio, I'd take the job (whether it paid or not). If I didn't know the person calling me, I'd simply decline.

The bottom line is to use your common sense. If you research the film/TV/commercial credits of the person who has contacted you (and who can't pay you), and you discover the individual doesn't have any credits, chances are he or she is all bark and no bite. Make sure you get paid first by those individuals. Likewise, if you research the film credits on a particular production designer who contacted you and wants you to work as a local, and you discover the designer's last four or five credits were block-buster movies, take the job.

We all have to eat and pay the bills, and working free doesn't provide that luxury. But I'm sure you've heard the expression, "A step back can lead to two steps forward." Rely on your common sense and instinct. Think outside the box. Consider the big picture. When starting out in the storyboard business, one of your goals is to set up opportunities for yourself.

When you receive that phone call for work, evaluate the offer. If it provides an opportunity to work for major players or a studio in Hollywood, take the job. If it offers you work with people you've never heard of, or who don't have any credits or a track record, make sure you get paid up front. There's nothing worse than getting burned.

Chapter fifteen

UNION vs NON-UNION

As a beginning storyboard artist, the topic of unions is extremely important and should not be overlooked. Nor should your union status be decided upon "down the road." If your career plans are to be a storyboard artist, now is the time to be seriously thinking about the union. There is a class of unions for the majority of film positions today. There is even a union for storyboard artists and production illustrators, depending on where you live. In Los Angeles, for example, the union is Local 790. For more information on your local unions and requirements for admission, contact the IATSE (The International Alliance of Theatrical Stage Employees) for a listing near you. IATSE is the labor union that represents technicians, artisans and crafts persons in the entertainment industry, including live theater, film and television production. You can get more information on the Internet at www.iatse.lm.com.

The purpose of IATSE is to protect artists like yourself from working for less than scale. Like the rules regarding minimum wage, the union makes sure you aren't receiving less than what you should be making. By joining the union, you become entitled to such services as health insurance, vacation pay and retirement pensions.

From a production standpoint, the union creates problems. Many producers and studios try to avoid paying the high, non-negotiable rates dictated by the union by producing their film/TV projects out of the Los Angeles area and under non-union status.

As you will discover from being a storyboard artist, there are only two types of film/TV assignments you will be asked to work on: union and non-union. For union work, you must be a member of the storyboard/illustrator union. If not, you can only work on non-union projects. A gray area surfaces when you are a union member and take non-union work. Since the union heavily discourages this and recommends you avoid it, if you find yourself needing to make money by taking a non-union job, I'd advise that you keep it quiet and make sure the union doesn't find out.

How does one get into the union? That's the most difficult part. In order to qualify for admission, using the Los Angeles based Local 790 as an example, you must have worked a minimum of 30 days on a union project. In order to do that, you need to get hired as a story-board artist/illustrator on a non-union project before it organizes to union status, which is the only way you can get on a union project to begin with.

When I was hired by Joel as his art department coordinator/illustrator on Paramount's The Temp, the production began as a non-union film. During the course of the movie, Paramount reorganized the production to a union picture. Since many of us were non-union hires, we were allowed to immediately qualify as union members. That's also why it was so important for me to receive a Production Illustrator credit rather than that of Art Department Coordinator. Because Joel was nice enough and had the authority to give me such a credit, and I had worked on the film for more than 30 days, I was now able to join the union and accept union work thereafter.

The only other way to get into the union or receive union work is to list your name with the union as a non-union member. Then when a production needs to hire a union illustrator, its representative will look at the list provided by the union. If all union members are busy or pass on the particular job, the production company is then allowed to hire non-union members.

The chances of this happening are very slim, so I recommend you hustle and try to get on a large non-union picture, and hope that the project reorganizes to union status. Of course, you can always take the director's assistant route on a union picture, although your days won't make you eligible for union status as an illustrator.

LESSON #15: Make sure you join the union as soon as you qualify. There's nothing worse than getting a phone call for storyboard work that you can't accept because you're not in the union.

What have we learned in this section on storyboards in action? Let's have a short review:

- A production designer prefers an experienced storyboard artist to a rookie. You have to believe in the existence of "the one" designer who will hire you because of your passion and artistic ability.
- Don't panic if you don't get hired immediately following an interview. Learn from your meeting, and prepare for the next one.
- Once you are hired, remember that production designers are your employers, your mentors and your references. They are a wealth of information.
- Your art department may be at home, or on location. Wherever it is, you need a functional area where you can focus on the job and do your best work.
- The director's vision is everything. Stay flexible, professional and open to criticism. Neatness and promptness count.
- Network! Use all the resources you can, including industry publications. The more you advertise, the more letters you write, the more you stay in contact with fellow crew members, and the more names and phone numbers you obtain – the more opportunities you create for more work.
- Most of us need to earn money to live. Let common sense be your guide. If a well-known production designer calls to offer you a non-paying job, consider what you might learn before turning down the work.
- The International Alliance Of Theatrical Stage Employees (IATSE) is a highly reputable union. It's difficult to get into, but once you've joined, you benefit from its protective arm. Join the union as soon as you qualify.

PART IV

READY FOR HOLLYWOOD?

Chapter Sixteen

BEFORE PACKING YOUR BAGS

Now that you have some professional experience under your belt, and a snappy portfolio to prove you're a serious illustrator, it's time to further your career as a storyboard artist.

If you want to be an artist merely as a hobby or for recreational purposes, then the pressure and willingness to continue shouldn't cause you any additional stress. You'll keep your day job and just draw on the side, maybe landing one or two assignments a month, giving you some extra money for the weekends.

But if you want storyboarding to be your full-time job and ultimately your one true profession, you will need a steady stream of work day after day, week after week, month after month and year after year. In other words, you will need to situate yourself in a geographical region where the demand for storyboarding is plentiful, thereby increasing your chances of getting work and remaining steadily employed.

For instance, if you live in a small farm town community where a movie comes into your area once in a blue moon, it will probably be very tough to stay busy as an entertainment illustrator year round. On the other hand, if you live in the greater metropolitan cities, specifically in New York, Los Angeles or Vancouver, B.C., the chances are much greater that you'll receive an ample amount of film and television opportunities. To sum it up in one simple sentence: YOU NEED TO GO WHERE THE WORK IS.

The toughest decision for me was to leave my family, friends and hometown of Seattle, Washington, to move back to Los Angeles, where I had gone to college to pursue a career in the entertainment industry. I had heard many horror stories about the thousands of individuals who had done what I was about to do, only to find themselves moving back home months later after falling on their faces and failing miserably.

I also knew that the entire city of "Angles" worked in the entertainment industry, and I would always be competing with hundreds of other professional and very talented artists who were also jockeying for positions in the marketplace. Nevertheless, I was willing to take that chance. I figured I would rather compete with others for the copious number of film projects available than starve while waiting for a film or television company to make its way into my hometown.

Before I actually loaded up my car to make the drive down south, I had to be serious and ready for the move. This brings up the most important point of the chapter: Don't even think about leaving home unless you've done all your homework and feel it would be in your best interest to move. Let me explain in more detail.

It's a given that you will have to travel to where the work is, if you don't already live there, to pursue a successful career in the storyboard industry. But deciding to wing it and create your plan of attack once you arrive in the new city is unwise. Traveling blind, trying to go with the flow is a sure-fire way of finding yourself without any work.

To succeed in the new city, preferably Hollywood, you first must create a game plan and stick diligently to your plan without deviating or giving up. Like a football coach who enters a game with a plan of attack, you need to make sure that you follow through each step until you achieve success.

When I left for Los Angeles, I created a solid game plan to follow. As a result, I remained steadily employed for seven years in Hollywood before deciding to conduct my business from Seattle. Let me share my game plan with you.

91

Before packing your bags, you need to line up job prospects. Don't wait until you get to Hollywood to line them up. Start before you leave. Then when you arrive, you will already be one step ahead of the competition. You'll have a handful of interviews to attend, saving you time and, most importantly, the money you have saved for this venture.

You will begin lining up your job prospects by making numerous phone calls and mailing an endless number of inquiry letters. Remember those crew lists you saved from the film projects you worked on? Open them and contact all of those who live in the area you're moving to, which, more than likely, will be Los Angeles.

Refresh their memory. Remind them where and when you worked with them and tell them that you'd like to get together for a cup of coffee once you arrive, in order to pick their brain about employment possibilities. Also, make sure you get a current copy of the Hollywood Creative Directory and the LA 411. In these books, you will find listings of every film studio and production company in the greater Los Angeles area. They are filled with who's who in the entertainment industry, with phone numbers and addresses. These are probably the best books, in my opinion, for introducing yourself and establishing initial contact. Before leaving Seattle, I purchased both of them.

The next step I took was to write a one or two page form letter introducing myself and informing the reader that I was a professional storyboard artist who had experience and was seeking an interview for an employment opportunity.

To give you an example of how many letters I had to write before I eventually was offered a job, consider this: Before leaving for Hollywood, I mailed 150 letters to various individuals at both film studios and production companies in the Los Angeles area. Of those 150 letters, I received 21 responses. Of those 21 responses, 8 were willing to set up an interview with me once I arrived in California. Eventually, from those 8 interviews, 2 offered me a job. One of these offers was an unpaid internship.

So you see, you have to play the numbers game when setting up interviews before you leave. If you think writing 10 or 12 letters while you're in LA is going to be enough, you're mistaken. You must think volume, and target as many people as you can, because you can clearly see what the response rate was to my personal inquiries. It's also a good idea to make yourself a chart that lists all recipients of your letter and what the associated responses were, keeping you organized and aware of who has responded and who has not. After all, 150 letters are a lot to track.

Dear (Production Designer's name):

Thank you for taking the time to review my material. Enclosed you will find work samples that demonstrate my ability for a position in the art department.

Currently, I just finished working on the feature film THE TEMP, which was filmed in Portland, Oregon. My title on this picture was Production Illustrator. The duties I performed included storyboards, production sketches, drafting and model making. Along with daily artwork, I played a vital role in the creative process. I designed and drafted major props that was featured in the film.

Besides my talent in art, I am also well educated. With a degree from the University of Southern California, I can communicate effectively and handle myself in a business-like manner. This allows me to solve multiple tasks with extreme efficiency to meet deadlines. I was also in charge of handling the art department petty-cash account for the film.

I would like very much to be a part of your upcoming project. Like I have proved on other films, I will be an asset to the art department and will prove my abilities listed above. Whether you need assistance in the art department or just need an intern, I am available. I am 24 years old and am trying to gain as much experience as I can. I have worked steadily in film for one full year and feel confident that I have the talent to help your department.

Please give me the chance that others have given me. I will prove that you have made the right choice.

Thank you again and I look forward to hearing from you.

Sincerely,

James O. Fraioli
Enclosures:

Here's a copy of my letter to a particular production designer

December 8, 1992

Mr. (First & Last name)
c/o Walt Disney Studio
500 South Buena Vista Street
Burbank, CA 91505

Dear Mr. (Last name):

Thank you for taking the time to read this letter. I also request that you please respond after you have read this, since the following information will be fresh in your mind. Thank you.

Ever since I was a small child, I thoroughly appreciated movie making. I marveled at the ability of creating films that would capture an audience and hold them to their seat. Consider films such as JAWS and STAR WARS. They demonstrate a perfectly orchestrated picture, which has the power to impact the viewing audience. What highly intrigues me is the combined levels of imagination and artistic energy that pours into these films. The production designer, accompanied by the art director and finely tuned illustrators, set designers and model makers, confirms the importance of the art department. To this day, the art department performs a vital role in making a film visually pleasurable to the observing audience. I discovered the recent release of DRACULA an excellent example of a creative and artistic art department. Combined with Coppola's vision, Thomas Sanders' rendition of Dracula's castle is extremely impressive and visually stimulating.

As a graduate of USC, I am continuing to follow my aspirations in film. My ultimate goal is to be the best storyboard artist in Hollywood while establishing long lasting relationships with the major film companies.

As of now, I am contributing my specialized art and creative skills to film projects that venture to the Northwest. With my professional storyboards, thumbnail and illustration expertise and proficiency in drafting, production companies contact me locally for my assistance. Avenue Pictures, hiring me only three months out of college, was a foreshadow of great events to come. Two months later, Paramount Pictures became aware of my artistic and imaginative talents. The company requested me to join their art department for the filming of, THE TEMP (soon to be released). Working four solid months on the picture, reinforces my belief that production companies are seeking and appreciating my contributions.

A copy of my letter which I mailed to 150 prospects before packing my bags for Hollywood

Pointing out the obstacles in my path, working in the Northwest doesn't allow me to work on films consistently. Although production companies travel to the Northwest to film, there is not enough work to remain steadily employed. Being just 24 years of age and bursting with energy and determination, the monthly gaps between movies are frustrating. Further, when production companies travel with their entire art department, this eliminates my chances to prove myself and build experience.

After reflecting more about my desires of contributing full-time to film, my decision is to relocate. I am leaving the beautiful Northwest so I will focus more intensely on my film endeavors. With experience, creativity and artistic talent, Los Angeles will be the favorable route to follow. Where various film projects occur year around, my opportunities will be far more plentiful. Being very familiar with the motion picture industry and Southern California, my perseverance will reward me with success in this highly competitive industry.

When I arrive to Los Angeles in January, I would appreciate the chance of any internship or position at Walt Disney. Please, take interest in me and recognize what I have already accomplished. My resume should be a prime indicator of greatness to come. I guarantee, along with intense work ethics, my friendly personality and business intellect will compliment my personal attributes.

Thank you for spending time reading and understanding this letter. Again, please respond about any internship or position at Walt Disney. I appreciate your quickest reply. I wish you the best.

Sincerely,

James O. Fraioli
Enclosure

Page 2

95

Once you have lined up a handful of interviews (5 or 6), you are ready to coordinate those days and times with your actual departure date. If you fly, make sure you have access to a car once you get into town. It is imperative that you have a car when beginning, because relying on public transportation to get you around, especially during the interview process, is asking for serious trouble —unless, perhaps, you are interviewing in New York City, which has great public transportation. Why set yourself up for failure before you even get the chance to interview?

The next question you should think about is, "Where are you going to live?" It's going to take some time to get situated and land some paying jobs. Making your home in a luxury apartment or a fine hotel will drain your finances faster than you can say, "I'm broke!" You must think of inexpensive alternatives.

Before I left, I made some calls to college friends, and eventually set up a room for two weeks at a friend's parent's house. If you don't have that advantage, don't worry. Talk to your folks or relatives. There's a good chance, for instance, someone you or your friends know lives in the Los Angeles area.

You're not asking this individual if you can be a permanent roommate. What you are asking for is a place to stay for a week, or two at most, until you complete your interviews. Then once the interviews are over, you can assess your situation and decide, based upon what was offered, if you should get an apartment and run with the bone, or ask your friend if you can stay a little longer.

Remember, your goal is to find work right away to further your career. Concentrate on the interviews you have lined up, and not on whether or not you can see the Hollywood sign from your bedroom window.

Finally, let's talk about your current financial status. Are you rich? Do you come from money? Or are you financially in debt and barely able to scrape gas money together to make a trip across country?

Regardless of your money situation, you need to think logically and rationally. If you are dirt poor and can't afford to make a major move to a new city, then don't do it — not yet anyway. Work on building up a little nest egg so you can set up shop once you have a few dollars in your pocket. As I mentioned previously, it's going to take a little while to get your feet on the ground and to start collecting paychecks. If you can't afford to live on your own for a month or two, don't leave home.

If you do have some money saved up, your trip to Hollywood will be much smoother. But you can not think of your road trip as a vacation. You are still leaving home to get yourself a job and to carve out a serious career. Believing that you're waving goodbye to go out and play is taking a road to disaster.

My advice is, don't worry, there's plenty of time for you to tell all your friends back home that you're working in the movie business and you just saw Leonardo DiCaprio on Sunset Boulevard. Right now, focus on the interviews you have set up and on making the best impression possible so you get hired. Leave everything else for later.

It's also to your best advantage, especially if you're one of those people who get easily distracted in new environments, to make a list of your goals along with a time-line in which to complete them. So many aspiring movie enthusiasts pack their bags and move to Hollywood every year with enormous dreams and the intention of making it big and becoming filthy rich. Yet, after a year or so, if they haven't already moved home, they suddenly find themselves bartending or waiting tables to pay next month's rent.

Don't be one of those people. If you do, you'll get stuck in a rut which is almost impossible to shake. Before leaving home, write down your goals, starting with the most important to least important. For example:

My goals

1. Make a chart or list of all scheduled interviews.

2. Secure living arrangements for the first couple of weeks until interviews are completed.

3. Attend all interviews and accept the best opportunity that is offered.

4. Secure a more permanent residence after accepting the best job offered.

5. Conserve my money and save for "rainy days." (Just because I landed my first job, doesn't mean I'm well on my way).

6. Re-evaluate goals after one year. Am I still on track? Am I still working in the entertainment industry? Am I making money? Am I establishing myself and meeting new people in the industry?

If you are ready to tackle a storyboard career as your main profession, do your homework before leaving home. Don't try and wing it once you arrive. You'll be asking for instant failure if you do.

LESSON #16: If you are hesitant and not sure if you want to make the move to where the work is, you're not ready for a career in the storyboard business. You must be 100% focused and determined. Otherwise, you may need to re-evaluate what you really want for a career.

Chapter Seventeen

ARRIVING IN "TINSEL TOWN"

If you have never set foot in Los Angeles, the entertainment capital of the world, the city can be a very intimidating place. The cars move fast. The people are always in a rush. And the city is very spread out. Unlike New York or Boston, where public transportation and subways are the means of getting around, Los Angeles relies on cars, and plenty of them. So many, in fact, that traffic is constant along the highways, coupled with a layer of smog which blankets the sky overhead as a result of the automotive pollution. Also, gas prices are high, insurance is expensive and pretty much everything in Southern California will appear pricey. So, why move there? You should know that answer. You've got to go where the work is. If you were a computer programmer you would probably do better in Seattle working for Microsoft. If you want to be an astronaut, chances are better you'd find a job in Florida, at NASA. If you want to be a storyboard artist in the entertainment industry, Los Angeles is the place to be.

Movie studios — Walt Disney, Warner Brothers, Paramount, Sony, Universal and Dreamworks — all reside in the Los Angeles area, along with hundreds of production companies, actors, actresses and film crews. The bottom line is, if you want to find work in film and television, "Tinsel Town" is where you should start.

Welcome to Los Angeles!

Santa Monica Pier

The Hollywood Hills

Chinese Mann Theatre

Once you arrive in Los Angeles with your car stuffed to the gills with your belongings, don't immediately subject yourself to a sudden panic attack because you're not familiar with anything. Remember the days when you were a kid and you were introduced to a new school? Those days when you didn't know anybody and everything seemed frightening and larger than life? Well, what eventually happened? After a short while, once you settled in, you made new friends, felt more comfortable and the last thing you wanted to happen was to leave that school — the same school you were afraid of attending in the first place.

Moving to Hollywood is a similar experience. It's all going to appear overwhelming at first, but once you are settled in, you'll be taking the horse by the reins, and finding, in fact, that Los Angeles is a pretty enjoyable place to live. I, for one, love the city and lived there for 10 years. In fact, I'm planning to move back, because I miss it so much.

When you finally arrive at wherever you are going to stay for a couple of weeks, remember you are still on a mission, and you must stick to your game plan. You are not on vacation. It is not time to hit Disneyland, even though you haven't been there since you were a kid. As I said before, there's plenty of time for all of that.

First and foremost, thank your parent's friends, your buddy, or whomever you're staying with, for allowing you to stay with them through your interviews. Show your gratitude with some flowers or a nice bottle of wine. Then, put your stuff away and get your hands on a map of the city.

Since you have five or six interviews lined up already, you need to know exactly where you are going because there's nothing worse than showing up late for an interview. In fact, you should arrive early, giving yourself plenty of time to think about how you want to conduct yourself and what appropriate questions you want to ask.

Once you have mapped out the locations for your interviews, pick up the telephone and confirm your appointments. Also, make sure to mention that you have just arrived in town, and that you were told to call as soon as you got in. This will make your interview sound more important, reducing the chances of having the meeting rescheduled. It is also beneficial, at this time, to review your portfolio, to make sure everything is in good order. You should also have a stack of résumés that have been printed on a quality, neutral-colored paper, along with a box of business cards.

Remember, you need to think like a professional. From the minute you walk in the door for an interview, you are being observed and judged by the interviewer. Make sure everything you do comes across as business-like and professional.

Finally, once your interviews are confirmed and there's a roof over your head for a week or two, you can check out the city for areas you may want to live should your job prospects work out. In my case, I was quickly offered a script-reading job at TriStar Pictures, my first job in Los Angeles. After my two weeks were up and I didn't have enough money for an apartment right away, I ended up taking a spare room in a basement of a small motel in Santa Monica. There, I lived alongside the maids for one full year while I worked my way into the movie industry. The room was completely embarrassing and very depressing, to say the least, but my circumstances made me work that much harder. A year later, I was able to move myself into a two-bedroom duplex overlooking the ocean in Manhattan Beach.

Living in the dark basement in Santa Monica

Manhattan Beach Lifestyle

Chapter Eighteen

INTERVIEWING DO'S & DON'TS

You're off to your first interview! You've confirmed your appointments, you have directions to where you're going, your portfolio is in the back seat of your car and you're ready to make a great impression. Time to knock them dead.

Your interview will be either an actual interview for an illustrating job, or an exploratory interview to meet with a particular individual so you can introduce yourself, find out what jobs are out there or what film projects are starting soon. Exploratory interviews are highly recommended if you don't know a lot of people in the industry, because they are a great way to meet new people who are in the position to hire you.

Before you attend your first interview, you'll want to consider some "Do's and Don'ts" regarding the interview process in the entertainment industry. I have written these words of advice based on experiences I've had in numerous interviews. I suggest that you read them now and review them again before walking into the office of your first interview.

INTERVIEWING DO'S

1. **Do** arrive on time. Showing up late never works in your favor. By the same token, don't arrive early. It's a sign that you are too eager. If you do arrive early, take a seat somewhere outside the office so that you can think about the interview prior to going in.

2. **Do** make sure that you have a clean, crisp copy of your résumé; that your portfolio is in order, with your most recent work first; and that you have a business card to leave behind. Keeping your résumé and reference list in folders shows that you are organized and pay attention to detail, while making sure your documents are protected.

3. **Do** demonstrate, right off the bat, that you are professional and serious about storyboarding. When presenting your portfolio, get excited and stand behind your work. After all, it represents the best of all your hard work. Prove to the interviewer you also have the energy, respect, and willingness to prove yourself. Revealing that you left home to pursue a career as a storyboard artist is another clear-cut sign that you're serious about your intentions.

4. **Do** ask questions. Find out how the interviewer started in the business, where he/she has worked, what film/TV projects are coming up, and whether there are any other positions the interviewer is looking to fill. Your goal in the interview is to get your name out there while searching for your ultimate job.

5. **Do** send a follow-up card thanking the individuals who met with you. It's also a good idea to drop them a line or letter down the road, staying in touch with them. Interviewers, most often, soon forget about you. Receiving a "refresher" letter usually jogs their memory. Timing is everything, and a position may need to be filled the same day the interviewer has received your follow-up letter.

INTERVIEWING DON'TS

1. **Don't** overdress. Unless you are seeking a job as an attorney or accountant, don't wear a suit to the interview. In general, the film industry is very casual. A pair of khakis and a polo shirt will do just fine. The key is to look nice and presentable. Otherwise, you'll give the wrong impression as soon as you walk in the door.

2. **Don't** ever walk into an interview and say "I need a job". When you sit down to an interview, the first question the interviewer usually asks is something to the effect of, "What can I do for you today?" Use this as an opportunity to plug your amazing abilitites. This is your moment to pitch yourself and present to the interviewer your wide range of skills. Give the interviewer a brief explanation of your storyboard capabilities and how you left home to further your career. This shows your admiration for the industry and passion as an artist. Mention that you wanted the interview in order to meet people, and you would like to find out what type of storyboard opportunities are out there. This is a tactful way of saying that you are looking for a job.

3. **Don't** present your portfolio unless you are asked to do so. Many times the interviewer will believe you can draw and would rather know more about you than what's sketched on paper. Others will ask to see your portfolio right away. Let the interviewer decide.

4. **Don't** ever lie in an interview. If you are asked if you can draft and you can't, say that you can't. Likewise, don't put any false film/TV credits on your résumé. The film industry is a tight community and many people know each other. If you put phony credits on your resume, eventually someone will call you on it. Avoid that embarrassment. It won't help your career at all.

In general, if you look and act professional, you will create a lasting impression. Avoid gimmicks or over anxious attitudes. Just go into the interview and don't leave until you've accomplished the following objectives:

• You have learned a little bit about the people you've met, what they do, and how they possibly could help you.

• You have received at least one lead on a possible job or film/TV project getting ready to start pre-production.

• You have left behind your resume, business card and maybe even a sample of your work (copies only, NO originals).

The more interviews you go on, the more people you will meet. The more contacts you make, the better your chances of finding work. Hollywood is an endless circle of networking and strategy. Use those elements to your advantage and you will find yourself storyboarding for dollars in no time.

Chapter Nineteen

THE SECRET ABOUT INTERNSHIPS

In this book, we have talked about how important it is for you to network and build contacts in order to increase your chances of finding work. Internships work in a very similar fashion. In fact, interning, especially in Hollywood, will increase your job opportunities more than you could ever imagine.

You might be thinking "Wait a minute, I've already gone to school. Isn't that the time to participate in internship programs?" My answer to that question is yes and no. Of course, interning while in college is a fantastic way of getting your feet wet, making the transition into the workplace easier for you once you have graduated. However, many people, like me, don't know what career path to pursue while in school. Commonly, it isn't until a year or two later that we decide what we really want to do, especially if we suddenly fall into a career we weren't expecting, as I had done.

To get a jumpstart on your storyboarding career, especially if you have made the decision to move to Los Angeles, interning, in my opinion, is the best way to make immediate contacts and receive a crash course on how the overall entertainment industry operates.

After I arrived in Los Angeles and I concluded my interviews, I quickly accepted a job as a script reader for producer Gary Foster at TriStar Pictures. I was excited to have landed something immediately and grateful to be working for a well-known producer (Short Circuit, Sleepless in Seattle), but the job wasn't helping with my overall goal of becoming a successful storyboard artist.

I was put in a room by myself, where I read scripts all day long, then returned home to my basement dwelling to write coverage on the material. After one month of reading and writing, I realized that I wasn't getting my face in front of anybody, and I knew I needed a different position — one that would allow me to meet more industry professionals. That's when I turned to interning.

With TriStar not accepting any internships at that time, I quickly contacted Human Resources at the Walt Disney Studio, where I had already had an exploratory interview. Since only a month had gone by, the department remembered me and informed me that there were several internships now available. I immediately jumped in my car to look into those opportunities.

Arriving at Disney, I sat down to discuss one internship in particular. The pay was very little, but I would be working for the location department which assisted on all the movies Walt Disney was producing. At the time, that was roughly 30 to 40 a year. Can you already see the possible opportunity here? And remember my security guard scenario? You always need to be thinking of the big picture.

I was told I would be working with all of the film commissions worldwide; dealing with numerous directors, producers and movie studio executives, who are the same people who hire storyboard artists; and getting familiar with the way locations are chosen for each movie. Immediately, I accepted the internship, after thanking Gary Foster for the opportunity. Remember, you never want to burn a bridge.

Technically speaking, an intern is any individual who is enrolled in school and receiving credits for a particular internship, which assists the student in graduating from an accredited college or university. An intern has to work a certain number of hours per week and be supervised while on the job.

The problem for me was that I had already gone to college and was now trying to pursue a career as a storyboard artist, with the immediate goal of meeting as many people as I possibly could. The last thing I wanted was to think about going back to school. Fortunately, I found a way around the system.

Talking with an internship coordinator at the least expensive community college in Los Angeles, I was informed that in order to qualify for an internship program, I had to be enrolled at the community college. I then found out that, in order to be enrolled at the college, I had to sign up for a minimum of one class, qualifying me as a student.

Quickly paying for an art class, which cost hardly any money in the scheme of things, I received my student ID card, which was what one needed to receive a Disney internship. Within days, I was interning at the "Mouse House" while taking an art class in the evenings to keep from getting rusty.

To wrap up my internship story, four months later, my intern supervisor at Disney told me about a great position that became available. The position was assisting the Executive Production Manager for the motion-picture department, who oversaw every movie hammered out by the studio. As the EPM's assistant, I would be in direct contact with the directors, producers, production designers and studio executives involved with the slate of movies. One month later, I interviewed and was awarded the job.

111

Again, always think of the big picture and strategically place yourself in the best position possible for greater opportunities. Had I stayed at TriStar, who can say what would have happened? But I didn't have the luxury, the money or the time to find out. I had moved to Hollywood with a limited budget and a time line in which to accomplish my goals. I had to move fast, and I had to move strategically.

Taking an internship to put myself in front of more people became the most important stepping stone towards my storyboarding career. As a result, after one year of assisting the Executive Production Manager at Disney, I had introduced myself to more than 25 directors, 50 producers and over 100 production designers. I never had to worry about finding a storyboard job after that. I have remained steadily employed until this very day. By the way, if you are curious about who took my assistant position after I had left Disney...you guessed it. Another intern.

Chapter Twenty

STORYBOARDING & NETWORKING

You probably understand by now that storyboarding is not all about drawing. In order to obtain work, you need to know who to get it from. That's the life of a freelance artist. If you are an antisocial person who likes to hide at home, your phone will never ring no matter how good of an artist you are. You must force yourself to get out of the house and introduce yourself to as many entertainment professionals as you can. In Hollywood, it's all about networking and "who you know." The more people you know, the more work you will get.

I know I may sound like a broken record, preaching over and over again about networking, but I can't stress the importance of the topic enough. Of every storyboard job I received, only one came from out of the blue — from someone I didn't know. All the other work I received was from people I had met or previously worked for. Had I not gotten out there and introduced myself, I would have starved many times over waiting for that "stranger" to call.

Hollywood is filled with many talented artists all looking for a way to beat the competition and get hired on a particular movie. One of your goals should be to outsmart the competition by finding and utilizing a unique competitive approach.

In my case, I knew my illustrations weren't the best in the business. I couldn't use my artistic talent as the determining factor which would set me apart from the competition. Instead, I relied on strategy and marketing myself in order to get my foot in the door. Realizing that my artistic talent would hold up if I were offered a storyboard job, my focus was more on finding and getting the work. And getting the work, in my opinion, starts with meeting as many people as you can.

Although interning at Disney's location department (which, unfortunately no longer exists) or assisting a motion-picture studio executive isn't a storyboard position, those particular jobs placed me higher up on the ladder of gainful employment. Taking those positions with the right people at the right company was my competitive edge.

LESSON #17: In order to succeed as a storyboard artist, you must get out and meet people!

Chapter Twenty-one

KEEP ON DRAWING AND
RISING TO THE TOP

To become a sought-after storyboard artist, your imagination, creativity and drawing skills need to ultimately impress the directors and production designers. Proving to them that you have what it takes will put you in the driver's seat when it comes down to negotiating your storyboard rate and other associated perks (rental car, housing, and per diem). The better you are as a storyboard artist, the more you can command for your work. It's that simple. However, in order to become the best, you need to keep drawing and sharpening your skills.

Moving to Los Angeles and building your network base can easily cause you to get sidetracked and suddenly forget about the drawing side of your career goal. Networking is so vital to finding work that, at times, you may forget that your actual drawings are what get you hired and keep you aboard a particular production.

While storyboarding in my tenure, I made it a point to draw every single week I was not working, so I wouldn't get rusty. It was easy to hone my craft and sharpen my skills while on a film, because I was forced to draw and deliver the best illustrations I could on a daily basis. But, when I was finished with a project and I was hustling to line up my next gig, that's when my artistic responsibilities slipped through the cracks.

My advice to you is: don't put yourself in that situation. If you have taken a job as an intern or have become a producer's assistant at a major studio, don't forget about your one true mission of becoming the best storyboard artist you can be. Go home after work and spend an hour each night, or at least every other night, drawing and sketching various people and objects in motion. If you didn't land a storyboard job right away, get your hands on a couple of good scripts and practice drawing scenes from the screenplays. Then if you are actually happy with something you drew, add it to your portfolio (but don't lie and say you worked on that particular project). Mention that you worked for a major film studio and you storyboarded on the side to not get rusty — another sign that you are passionate about your work.

Are you clear about the crucial elements that will make or break your storyboard career? To summarize, here's a list of what you must never forget:

Crucial Elements to Remember

- Before you pack your bags, decide what you really want to do, and where you need to go to do it.
- Make a game plan, and stick to it. Send lots of letters. Line up job prospects before you go. Get copies of the Hollywood Creative Directory and LA 411.
- Pre-determine what transportation and housing you'll need for the amount of time you'll be job-searching. Wherever you live, write your goals on paper, so you can see them every day.
- When interviewing, arrive on time with several copies of your clean, crisp resume and an organized portfolio. Send a thank-you follow-up note to the individuals who take the time to meet with you.
- You may want to consider an internship. It can have remarkable benefits if you get to work with reputable people. Consider the "big picture."
- Get out there and meet people! The more you meet, the more you improve your chances to get work. Discover your competitive strengths! What do you do best? How can you best market yourself to get in the door?
- Never stop working on your craft. The faster and more accurately you can draw, the better you'll become. Always think about camera angles and your director's point of view. Keep your Polaroid handy.

- Join the Storyboard/Illustrator union the first chance you get. Always be friendly and act professionally.
- Make sure you're 100% focused and determined. Never give up!

I hope, after you have read this book, you understand a lot more of what is involved in having a career in storyboarding within the entertainment industry. Storyboarding was a lot of fun for me. I am fortunate to have some great mentors along the way who helped steer me in the right direction when I found myself veering off the main road.

The primary purpose for me in writing this book is to mentor young artists, like yourself, who are excited and willing to give storyboarding a shot. I understand how difficult it can be when you're just beginning and how important it is to receive support to push yourself to continue. I hope this book has helped you do that.

Keep this book with you wherever you go. Think of it as your personal mentor. Re-read it when you're drawing your first set of storyboards. Re-read it when you're considering moving to Hollywood to pursue your storyboard career. Re-read it when you're on a film set illustrating for the director. Maybe one day, you too will write a book about your adventures as a storyboard artist.

Until then, keep your chin up and your pencil sharpened. I wish you the very best in all of your storyboard endeavors. Remember, you can do anything you set your mind to. Now, set down this book, pick up that pencil and start drawing.

I'll be looking for your name when I go to the movies!

APPENDIX:
Important Phone Numbers to Keep in Your Pocket

<u>Name</u>	<u>Phone Number</u>
ABC Studios	310-557-7777
CBS Studios	323-575-2345
DreamWorks SKG	818-733-7000
Fox	310-369-1000
NBC Studios	818-840-4444
Paramount Pictures	323-956-5000
Sony Pictures	310-244-8000
Universal Studios	818-777-1000
Walt Disney Studio	818-560-1000
Warner Brothers Studio	818-954-6000

<u>Other Resources</u>

Association of Film Commissioners International (AFCI)	323-462-6092
Creative Directory	800-815-0503
Daily Variety	800-552-3632
The Hollywood Reporter	323-525-2000
IATSE (Local 790 – Production Illustrators)	818-784-6555
Locations Magazine	
Los Angeles Film Commission	213-957-1000
Los Angeles 411	800-545-2411

BIOGRAPHY

James O. Fraioli is a graduate of the University of Southern California. He began his film career working on the Jeff Bridges film, AMERICAN HEART. After completing other assignments on THE TEMP, SON-IN-LAW and the Super Bowl XXVII Half-Time Show, he moved to production, joining forces with a noted producer at Tri-Star. Next, Fraioli joined Walt Disney Studios as an associate to the executive production manager, where he helped to oversee more than 20 feature films, including THE JOY LUCK CLUB, CRIMSON TIDE and MR. HOLLAND'S OPUS. After building a successful relationship with Disney and other major studios, he returned to free-lance production and storyboard illustration. He worked on the Fox TV series FORTUNE HUNTER, then with high-profile directors such as Steve Oedekerk on ACE VENTURA: WHEN NATURE CALLS, William Dear on WILD AMERICA AND Academy Award winner Tom Schulman (DEAD POETS SOCIETY) on EIGHT HEADS IN A DUFFEL BAG. Fraioli also assisted on Disney's BELOVED. Fraioli currently resides in Seattle, Washington, where he runs his production company, Whiteshark Entertainment. In addition to this book, he has written a murder-mystery novel. Having produced promotional videos for high-profile clients, as well as TV pilots, his next film shoot is in Cape Town, South Africa.

For more information
Please visit
www.whiteshark.net

GLOSSARY:
Speaking the Film and Storyboard Language

Above-the-Line
Refers to the creative elements of a production. Usually the writer, producer, director and actors/actresses. In budgets, these elements appear first, followed by a line dividing them from below-the-line.

Action
"Action" is called during filming, indicating the start of a current take.

Actor/Actress
The "talent" who plays the role of a character in the script.

Added scenes
Material, shots, sequences, or scenes written into a script during principal filming or after its completion.

Aerial Shot
An extremely high angle view of a subject usually taken from a crane or high stationary object. Also may refer to a shot taken from an airplane or helicopter.

Angle
Relationship between the camera and the subject(s) of the shot.

Animation/Animator
Process of creating (or person responsible for) the illusion of motion by creating individual frames, as opposed to filming naturally occurring action at a regular frame rate.

Art Department
Crew concerned with visual artistry of a production. Members of art department include: production designer, art director, draftsman, leadman, production buyer, property master, set dresser, special effects supervisor, and others.

Art Director
Individual who oversees the artists and crafts people who build sets. Reports to the production designer.

Associate Producer
Producer who shares responsibility for creative and business issues. Usually works closely with post-production.

Atmosphere
Tone or dimension added to the action by concrete or nebulous qualities or elements such as rain, wind, heat, cold, danger, spookiness, tranquility.

Backdrop
Artificial background, usually painted on a cyclorama, curtain, or flats, used to achieve the effect of a natural environment such as a forest, beach, mountains, or other landscape in a shot or sequence.

Backend
Film's profit from theater ticket sales, video rentals, and ancillary markets.

Background Artist
Individual responsible for designing or constructing the art placed at the rear of a set.

Beat
Directional word used to indicate a pause in an actors speech or action of a sequence.

Below-the-line
Refers to the technical elements of the production staff. Appears beneath the above-the-line elements on a production budget.

Block/Blocking
Rehearsal to determine the position and movement of the camera, actors, and crew during a particular shot or scene.

Blockbuster
Movie which is a huge financial success.

Body Double
A body which is used for "doubling" an actor's body in certain scenes; i.e.: nudity shot.

Box Rental
A fee or allowance paid to a crewmember for providing his/her own equipment for use in a production.

Breakdown Script
Detailed list of all items, people, props and equipment required for a shoot on a day-by-day basis.

Budget
Funds required to produce a film or television production, derived by combining all projected expenses for equipment, salaries, locations, travel, and all other above-the-line and below-the-line production costs.

Call Sheet
Listing of what actors will be required for which scenes, and when they will be required.

Camera Angle
The viewpoint chosen from which to photograph a subject.

Camera Crew
Crewmembers directly involved with operation of the camera. Individual job titles include: clapper-loader, camera operator, assistant cameraman, director of photography, focus puller, grip, key grip, dolly grip, additional camera.

Cast
A collective term for the actors appearing in a particular movie.

Change Pages
When a script is being edited during production, changes are distributed to actors and the filmmakers on "change pages," which are usually a different color from the original pages of the script.

Cinematographer
Individual with expertise in the art of capturing images either electronically or on film stock through the application of visual recording devices and the selection and arrangement of lighting.

Close-up
Shot in which the subject is larger than the frame; approximately from the top of chest to top of head.

Co-Producer
Producer who has equal responsibility for the completion of a project.

Continuity
Degree to which a movie moves consistently without error or jump-cuts.

Coverage (production)
An indeterminate number of detailed shots intended to be intercut with a more general master shot or scene.

Credit
The authorship given to a written work in the entertainment industry. For film: "Story by," "Screenplay by," and "Written by." For TV: "Created by","Story by," and "Teleplay by."

Crew/crew members
Collective term for anyone involved with the production of a movie who does not appear in the movie.

Cut
In filming, to change from one shot to another immediately. In directing, called by the director to stop action by the performers, camera, and audio equipment. In film editing, to eliminate unwanted portions, visual or audio, of a film.

Dailies
First positive prints made from the negatives photographed on the previous day.

Day Out of Days
A form designating the workdays for various cast or crewmembers of a given production.

Deal Memo
A form which lists the pertinent details of salary, guaranteed conditions, and other essentials of a work agreement negotiated between a member of the cast or crew and a production company.

DGA
Directors Guild of America. A union which represents directors, assistant directors and production managers.

Director
Principal creative artist on a movie set.

Director of Photography
Cinematographer who is ultimately responsible for the process of recording a scene in the manner desired by the director.

Dissolve
Editing technique whereby the images of one shot are gradually replaced by the images of another.

Dolly
Small truck which rolls along dolly tracks carrying the camera and some camera crewmembers to get a steady, continuous shot.

Draftsman
Individual who creates the plans for set construction.

Dutch Angle
A process in which a camera is angled so that the horizontal frame line is not parallel to the horizon.

Establishing Shot
Usually a long, wide shot showing much of the location, intended to inform the audience about an upcoming scene.

Executive Producer
Producer who is not involved in any technical aspects of the film-making process, but who is responsible for the overall production, usually handling business and legal issues.

Exterior / EXT.
Used in a slug line of a script, indicates that the scene occurs outdoors.

Extra
Individual who appears in a movie where a non-specific, non-speaking character is required, usually as part of a crowd or in the background of a scene.

Extreme Close-up/ECU
Shot in which the subject is much larger than the frame. Provides more detail than a close-up.

Extreme Long Shot
Camera cue in direction used to describe a shot taken a long distance from the subject.

Fade
Smooth, gradual transition from a normal image to complete blackness (fade out), or vice versa (fade in).

Fade IN
First words typed in a script. Literally mean "to begin."

Fade OUT
Last words in a script which mean "the end."

Flashback
Scene that breaks the chronological continuity of the main narrative by depicting events which happened in the past.

Flashforward
Scene that breaks the chronological continuity of the main narrative by depicting events which happen in the future.

Foreground
Objects or action closest to the camera.

Format
Describes the equipment and film or tape used. Examples for film: 8mm, Super 8, 16mm, 35mm. For video: VHS, HI-8, Beta.

Freeze Frame
Optical printing effect whereby a single frame is repeated to give the illusion that all action has stopped.

Green Light
To give a film project the studio backing and financing to begin principal photography.

Guerrilla Producer
One who produces an effective video on a shoestring budget.

Hot Set
Set on which a scene is in the process of being shot; so labeled to indicate that it should not be changed or disturbed.

Independent Film /Indie
Movie not produced by a major studio.

Insert
Close-up shot of an object, often produced by the second unit.

Interior/ INT.
Used in a slug line, indicates that the scene occurs indoors.

Jump Cut
Cut involving an interruption to the continuity of time.

Letterboxing
Technique of shrinking the image just enough so that its entire width appears on a TV screen, with black areas above and below the image.

Line Producer
Producer who is responsible for managing every person and issue during the making of a film.

Location Filming
Filming that occurs at a place not constructed specifically for the production.

Majors
Major Hollywood movie producer/distributor studios (MGM/UA, 20th Century Fox, Sony Pictures, Warner Bros, Paramount Pictures, Universal, and Disney).

Match Cut
A transition from one scene to another matching the same or a similar subject within the frame.

Matte Artist
Individual who creates artwork (usually for the background of a shot) which is included in the movie either via a matte shot or optical printing.

Matte Shot
Photographic technique whereby artwork — usually on glass — from a matte artist is combined with live action.

Medium Shot (MS)
A camera angle often used to describe a shot of a character from the waist up.

Montage
A rapid succession of shots, achieved through the use of many short shots.

MOS
Silent filming method.

Pan
The action of rotating a camera about its fixed axis.

Post-Production
Work performed on a movie after the end of principal photography.

Pre-Production
Arrangements made before the start of filming; script editing, set construction, location scouting, and casting.

Principal Photography
The filming of major or significant components of a movie which involve lead actors.

Producer (Film)
The chief of a movie production in all matters, except the creative efforts of the director; raising funding, hiring key personnel, and arranging for distributors.

Producer (TV)
Usually a current or former writer who has successfully written for a number of years as a staff member on a show and is now responsible for the creative aspects of the show.

Production Assistant
Individual responsible for various odd jobs, such as stopping traffic, acting as a courier, fetching items from craft service, and many others.

Production Company
Company headed by a producer, director, actor/actress, or writer for the purpose of creating general entertainment products such as motion pictures, television shows, commercials, and multimedia.

Production Date
Refers to the phase of movie-making during which principal photography occurs.'

Production Designer
Artist responsible for designing the overall visual appearance of a movie.

Production Illustrator
Individual responsible for drawing the storyboards and anything else that needs to be drawn during the production of the movie.

Production Manager
Individual responsible for practical matters such as ordering equipment and getting near-location accommodations for the cast and crew.

Production Schedule
Detailed plan of the timing of activities associated with the making of a movie, of particular interest to production managers.

Prop
Object on the set used by an actor, such as phones, guns, or cutlery.

Reaction Shot
Shot of a person reacting to dialogue or action.

Scene
Continuous block of storytelling either set in a single location or following a particular character.

Screenplay
A script written to be produced as a movie. Normally between 95-120 pages.

Second Unit
Small, subordinate crew responsible for filming shots of less importance, such as inserts, crowds, and scenery.

Set
An artificial environment constructed to make filming easier, that appears natural when viewed from the camera angle.

Set Designer
Individual responsible for translating a production designer's vision of the movie's environment into a set that can be used for filming.

Shooting Schedule
Production schedule for shooting a film with the scenes from a script grouped together and ordered with production considerations in mind.

Shooting Script
Script, from which a movie is made, that includes scene numbers, camera angles, inserts, and certain director/cinematographer input.

Short Subject/ Short
Movie that is shorter than 60 minutes.

Slug Line/Slug
A header appearing in a script before each scene or shot detailing the location, date, and time the following action.

Steadicam
Camera attached to a camera operator via a mechanical harness which reduces or eliminates the unsteadiness of the operator's motion.

Stock Footage
Footage from other films that are used in a production. Also known as library shots.

Take
An individual shot.

Tilt
Rotating the camera either up or down.

Tracking Shot
The action of moving a camera along a path parallel to the path of the object being filmed.

Trades
Newspapers that report the daily or weekly entertainment news of the entertainment industry; The Hollywood Reporter & Daily Variety.

Unit Production Manager
Executive who is responsible to a senior producer for the administration of a particular movie.

Whip Pan
Extremely fast pan, incorporating much motion blur.

Wipe
Editing technique in which images from one shot are fully replaced by the images of another, delineated by a definite border that moves across or around the frame.

Wrap
To finish shooting, either for the day or the entire production.

Zoom
Shot in which the magnification of the objects by the camera's lenses is increased (zoom in) or decreased (zoom out/back).

Film Directing: Shot by Shot

Visualizing from Concept to Screen

Steven D. Katz

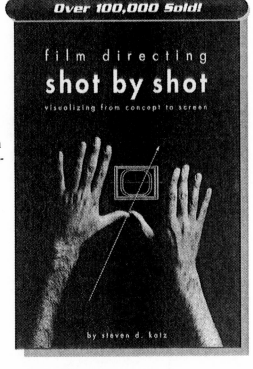

Over 100,000 Sold!

film directing

shot by shot

visualizing from concept to screen

by steven d. katz

An instant classic since its debut in 1991, "Film Directing: Shot by Shot" and its famous blue cover is one of the most well-known books on directing in the business, and is a favorite of professional directors as an on-set quick reference guide. This international bestseller is packed with visual techniques for filmmakers and screenwriters to expand their stylistic knowledge.

Contains in-depth information on shot composition, staging sequences, pre-visualization, depth of frame, camera techniques, and much more.

Contains over 750 storyboards and illustrations, including never before published storyboards from Steven Spielberg's *Empire of the Sun*, Orson Welles' *Citizen Kane*, and Alfred Hitchcock's *The Birds*.

> *"(To become a director) you have to teach yourself what makes movies good and what makes them bad. John Singleton has been my mentor…he's the one who told me what movies to watch and to read the book* Shot by Shot.*"*
> **Ice Cube**, Rap artist, actor and filmmaker
> Quoted in *The New York Times*, April 16, 1998

Doubleday Stage & Screen Book Club Selection
Movie Entertainment Book Club Selection

$24.95, ISBN: 0-941188-10-8
370 pages, 7 x 10, 750+ illus.
Order # 7RLS

Both Katz books only $44

Film Directing: Cinematic Motion

Steven D. Katz

This follow-up to the phenomenally popular "Shot by Shot" is a practical guide to common production problems encountered when staging and blocking film scenes. Includes discussions of scheduling, staging without dialog, staging in confined spaces, actor and camera choreography, sequence shots, and more. Also contains interviews with well-known professionals such as legendary indie director John Sayles, cinematographer Allen Daviau (*E.T.*, *Empire of the Sun*), and Visual Effects Coordinator Van Ling (*The Abyss, Terminator 2*).

STEVEN D. KATZ is an award-winning filmmaker with over 25 years of experience in the fields of writing, directing, and editing. His award-winning short "Protest" is screening at film festivals around the world, and he is currently working on his newly launched entertainment Web site Pitch TV (www.pitchtv.com).

$24.95, ISBN: 0-941188-14-0
200 pages, 7 x 10, hundreds of illustrations
Order # 6RLS

Save 12% when you order both books together!
Only $44.00 for both books
Order # KatzB

Directing 101

Ernest Pintoff

Written by one of the most respected and versatile filmmakers in the business, this unique book takes a broad look at the process of directing. All the basics are here, from selecting and acquiring material to communicating with cast and crew, budgeting, production planning and filming techniques. A veteran of the movie business for nearly five decades, Pintoff shares the wisdom he's gleaned from years of working as a film, animation and TV director, and encourages students and professionals alike to experience the benefits of looking outside of the movie industry for inspiration.

ERNEST PINTOFF is an Oscar™ winning director, producer, writer, and teacher with over 40 years of experience in the entertainment industry. His long list of credits includes the award-winning animated short *Flebus* and the television series *MacGuyver*, *The Bionic Woman* and *The Dukes of Hazzard*. Pintoff, who resides in Los Angeles, has also taught filmmaking in various schools throughout the US and Europe.

Movie Entertainment Book Club Selection
Doubleday Book Club Selection

$16.95, ISBN 0-941188-67-1
216 pages, 6 x 9, Bibliography, Subject Index
Order # 40RLS

MICHAEL WIESE PRODUCTIONS
11288 Ventura Blvd., Suite 621
Studio City, CA 91604
1-818-379-8799
kenlee@earthlink.net
www.mwp.com

Write or Fax
for a
free catalog.

Please send me the following books:

Title   Order Number (#RLS___)   Amount

_____ _____

_____ _____

_____ _____

_____ _____

SHIPPING   _____

California Tax (8.25%)   _____

TOTAL ENCLOSED _____

Please make check or money order payable to
Michael Wiese Productions

(Check one) ___ Master Card ___Visa ___Amex

Credit Card Number_____

Expiration Date_____

Cardholder's Name_____

Cardholder's Signature_____

SHIP TO:

Name_____

Address_____

City_____State_____Zip_____

HOW TO ORDER
CALL
24 HOURS
7 DAYS A WEEK

CREDIT CARD
ORDERS
CALL
1-800-833-5738

OR FAX YOUR
ORDER
818-986-3408

OR MAIL THIS
FORM

SHIPPING
ALL ORDER MUST BE PREPAID
UPS GROUND SERVICE
ONE ITEM- $3.95
EACH ADDTLN ITEM, ADD $2

EXPRESS -3 BUSINESS DAYS
ADD $12 PER ORDER

OVERSEAS
SURFACE - $15.00 EACH ITEM
AIRMIAL - $30.00 EACH ITEM

Printed in the United States
16124LVS00007B/178-237